BIG KNITS BIG NEEDLES

BIG KNITS BIG NEEDLES

Helgrid van Impelen

Photography: Katja Schubert

Contents

Big Needles

FAST RESULTS

The joy of knitting begins before you cast on a single stitch. Can you imagine a more inviting sight than a basket filled to overflowing with balls of thick mohair, luxurious alpaca, sleek silk, or flawless, matte cotton, in shades ranging from subtle natural hues to vivid, eye-popping colors? And stuck in the middle of this fleecy mix, there is a pair of smooth, chunky bamboo needles, just waiting for you to pick them up and put them to use.

Then, when you take up those needles and start to work, you know you can put aside the worries of the day and lose yourself in an activity that is both practical and creative. The pleasure of knitting is seasoned by the anticipation of seeing—and feeling—the finished article.

And best of all is that sense of achievement you have when friends admire a finished creation, and you can say, "I knitted it myself!"

This book will help you to achieve all this quickly and easily, because—depending on the project—the chunky yarns and big needles mean that you can achieve real success in just a few hours.

In the first section, "City knits," the focus is on sophisticated designs with subtle color accents—perfect choices for shopping, visiting a gallery, or meeting friends for lunch. "Country style" has a rustic flavor, with natural shades of beige, chocolate, and eggplant. You'll find capes, ponchos, and cardigans to keep out the chill in style. "Home comforts" is a delicious collection of delicate pastel shades, silky, sensuous yarns, and relaxed styles, tailor-made for cozy evenings curled up on the sofa.

Whether you are a beginner, a returner, or an expert, there's something for you here. Each project's difficulty level is graded from 1 to 4—just look for the balls of yarn in the materials box at the start of each project. And, in addition to easy-to-follow patterns and inspirational photos, you'll also find plenty of tips and useful information on tools, techniques, and yarns.

I wish you inspiration, relaxation—and fun!

Helgrid van Impelen

Tools and equipment

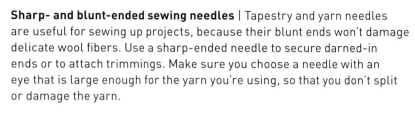

Sharp- and blunt-ended sewing needles | Tapestry and yarn needles are useful for sewing up projects, because their blunt ends won't damage delicate wool fibers. Use a sharp-ended needle to secure darned-in ends or to attach trimmings. Make sure you choose a needle with an eye that is large enough for the yarn you're using, so that you don't split or damage the yarn.

Cable needle | Cable needles have a point at each end and a small, V-shaped bend, or kink, in the middle. The kink prevents stitches from sliding away when knitting cable patterns. Cable needles are available in various sizes; select needles that are closest in size to the needles you are using for the rest of your knitting.

Stitch holder | You should always try to keep enough stitch holders handy—they are especially useful when you need to set aside stitches at shoulders, necklines, or pockets to work on later. If you run out of stitch holders, you can use spare double-pointed needles, but be careful, since stitches can easily slide off needles without stitch stoppers.

Row counter | A row counter helps you to keep track of how many rows you have completed as you knit. You can slip it onto one of your needles or attach it to your work with a safety pin. Some counters have to be manually changed every time you finish a row; others are just "clicked" at the end of each row. Either way, they only work if you remember to use them!

Tape measure | Before you start a project, use a tape measure to take the body measurements of the person you are knitting for, or to compare the measurements of the project with an existing article of clothing that you know fits well. During the project, keep a tape measure handy to check gauge or to measure your knitting.

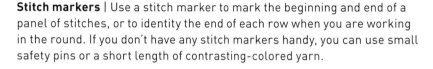

Stitch markers | Use a stitch marker to mark the beginning and end of a panel of stitches, or to identity the end of each row when you are working in the round. If you don't have any stitch markers handy, you can use small safety pins or a short length of contrasting-colored yarn.

Scissors | You should always keep a small pair of good-quality needlecraft scissors handy, for cutting off yarn and trimming ends. Sharp, short-bladed scissors are best: they allow you to snip really close to the work, keeping darned-in ends neater when you finish a seam.

Double-pointed needles | Designed so that stitches can be slipped on and off at both ends, double-pointed needles (also called dpns) are used for circular knitting, or for tubes. They are short needles that can only accommodate a small number of stitches, making them the best option for knitting very narrow tubes, such as gloves or socks. Many knitters find that wooden and bamboo double-pointed needles are easier to work with as they are less slippery than metal or plastic needles.

Circular needles | Circular needles consist of a flexible cord that attaches to needles at either end. They are mainly used for knitting tubular items, such as hats, socks, or seamless sleeves. You can work a piece of flat knitting with circular needles; just turn your needles around after every row instead of working in the round. Long circular needles are also used for knitting wide or heavy items, such as blankets, because the weight of the work is taken by the cord and it can sit in your lap, rather than hanging off the ends of standard needles, putting strain on your wrists. This makes it more comfortable to knit as your work gets heavier. Interchangeable circular needles are worth investing in if you find you prefer to use circular needles for all your projects. Circular needle sets are made up of connecting tubes of various lengths and a selection of different-sized needles.

Before you begin

TIPS FOR SUCCESS

Before you begin | While it is true that thick yarns are easier to knit and that even beginners can achieve success in a short space of time, you will enjoy the projects more and achieve even better results if you keep in mind a few basic guidelines.

Plan for success | If you are new to working with thick yarns, think about which styles suit your figure and choose an appropriate pattern. Thick yarns can give a bulkier result than thinner ones. So, for larger sizes, opt for casual, one-size styles and avoid designs with tight sleeves or small armholes. For a flattering outline, go for patterns with few seams. If you are not sure which size to choose, compare the pattern measurements with those of a similar garment from your wardrobe that you know fits well.

Yarn quantities | The chunkier the yarn and the larger the needles, the more yarn you will need. Buying a less expensive yarn does not always turn out to be the bargain it seemed to be. A higher-quality, more expensive yarn often keeps its looks longer and is more durable than a cheaper option. Choose a classic style and colorway and enjoy wearing your garment for years to come.

Chunky yarns are heavy | Keep in mind that chunky yarns can be quite heavy once they are knitted up. A knitted coat or long jacket will always stretch a little because of the sheer weight of the yarn. This has been taken into account when calculating the lengths of the designs in this book.

Alta Moda for best results | The Alta Moda yarns from Lana Grossa used for some of the designs in this book are particularly good for very big stitches. The yarn structure looks like a thinner version of a tube from a French knitter. This gives maximum volume from a comparatively small quantity of yarn. Knitwear made from Alta Moda feels lighter and airier than those made from spun yarns but is just as warm and cozy.

Stay loose | Choose larger rather than smaller needle sizes and remember to keep your knitting loose. Particularly fleecy yarns should be knitted with very big stitches. If the stitches are too close together, the surface can look slightly matted, the yarn will not look its best, and the finished garment will be stiff.

Avoid seams | Knit as far as possible in a single piece, so that you avoid seams in your garment. Thick seams can be ugly and uncomfortable, they add bulk, and can give a lumpy outline. Always knit sleeves on a set of circular or double-pointed needles. Make jackets without side seams and knit shoulder seams together, rather than sewing them.

Less is more | Working with thick yarns and big needles will give your knits a strong visual appeal. There is often no need for fancy stitches—all you need to create a striking, trendy garment are a few basic knitting techniques and a strong sense of color. If you do choose to use a fancy stitch, don't make it too detailed or fussy, or it will lessen the visual impact of your item.

City knits

AS YOU SOAK UP THE LAST OF THE FALL SUN AT YOUR FAVORITE
SIDEWALK CAFÉ, ALL YOU NEED TO KEEP OUT THE CHILL IS A
FROTHY CAPPUCINO AND A WARM, FLEECY KNIT!

Cosmopolitan color

RIBBED SWEATER WITH MATCHING MITTENS

FOR THE SWEATER

GAUGE
7 stitches and 26 rows in fisherman's rib on US17 (12mm) needles = 4in (10cm) square.

STITCHES
Fisherman's rib | In all rows slip the purl stitches purlwise, yarn over needle, and knit the plain stitches together with the yarn over from the previous row. Knit as loosely as possible.
Edge stitch | Work the first and last stitches of every row knitwise.

Back and front | The back and front are identical. Cast on 35 stitches and work the first row as a wrong-side row as follows:
Knit 1 purl 1 alternately, ending with a knit stitch.
Continue in fisherman's rib:
Row 1: (right-side row): Knit 1 (edge stitch), *knit 1, yarn over, slip 1 purlwise*; repeat from * to *, ending with knit 1 and 1 edge stitch.
Row 2: (wrong-side row): Knit 1, * yarn over, slip 1 purlwise, knit 1 together with the yarn over in the previous row*; repeat from * to *, ending with yarn over, slip 1 purlwise, and 1 edge stitch.
Row 3: Knit 1, *knit 1 together with the yarn over in the previous row, yarn over, slip 1 purlwise *; repeat from * to * ending with knit 1 together with yarn over in the previous row and 1 edge stitch.

RIBBED SWEATER WITH MATCHING MITTENS
One size
Style: loose, but not oversized

MATERIALS
- 10 balls Lana Grossa Alta Moda Super Baby (66yd/50g; 67% wool, 30% alpaca, 3% polyamide) in orange red (col. 18) for sweater and leftover yarn for mittens (single yarn)
- 2 balls Lana Grossa Merino Air (142yd/130m/50g; 90% wool, 10% polyamide) in col. 003, anthracite (yarn will be worked double) for mittens
- US17 (12mm) circular needles, 24 and 32in (60 and 80cm) long, for sweater
- Set of US10½ (7mm/UK2) double-pointed needles for mittens
- Stitch holder or spare needle

Repeat rows 2 and 3 until work measures 21½in (55cm).

Shoulders | When work measures 21½in (55cm), cast off the outer 10 stitches at both edges and knit the stand-up collar on the central 15 stitches.

Collar | Work 2⅜in (6cm) in fisherman's rib and cast off all stitches loosely.

Join the shoulder and collar seams | Place the front and back right sides together and on each side sew the shoulder and collar together in a single, continuous seam.

Armholes | Measure 8¼in (21cm) down from the shoulder seams and mark the position of the armholes.

Sleeves | Cast on 17 stitches and start with a wrong-side row: work 1 row in knit 1 purl 1 rib, starting with knit 1.
Then work in fisherman's rib pattern, as described for the back and front.

Sleeve increases | Increase 1 stitch at each end of every 6th right-side row 6 times (29 stitches). Increase by working make 1 between the first two stitches and the last two stitches of the row by picking up the horizontal strand between the stitches and knitting into the back of it. When work measures 19½in (50cm), cast off all stitches loosely. The sleeve length is generous, so that the cuffs can be rolled up.

Finishing | Sew the top edge of the sleeve to the back and front between the markers. Then, starting from the bottom edge, join the front and back together and the sleeve seam from the armhole down to the bottom edge in one continuous seam. Repeat on the other side of the garment. Darn in all the ends.

FOR THE MITTENS
GAUGE
12 stitches and 16 rows in stockinette stitch with double yarn on US10½ (7mm/UK2) needles = 4in (10cm) square.

STITCHES
Stockinette stitch in rounds | Knit all stitches.
Rib border | Knit 1 purl 1 alternately.

Border | With double yarn in anthracite and the set of double-pointed needles, cast on 20 stitches and distribute evenly between the needles. Work 3½in (9cm) in rounds in single rib. Work 3 rounds in stockinette stitch, then start increasing for the thumb.

Thumb | 1st increase: increase 1 stitch at each side by knitting into the strand between the first two stitches and the last two stitches of the round. Knit these stitches through the back of the loop in the next round to prevent holes from appearing in the work.
Work 2 rounds in stockinette stitch.
2nd increase: increase 1 stitch at each side by knitting into the strand between the second and third stitches and between the second and third stitches from the end of the round. Knit these stitches through the back of the loop in the next round to prevent holes from appearing in the work.
Work 2 rounds in stockinette stitch.
3rd increase: increase 1 stitch at each side by knitting into the strand between the third and fourth stitches and between the third and fourth stitches from the end of the round (26 stitches). Knit these stitches through the back of the loop

in the next round to prevent holes from appearing in the work.
Work 2 rounds in stockinette stitch.

Thumb | Slip the first 3 stitches of the first needle and the last three stitches of the last needle onto safety pins.

Hand | Join the remaining 20 stitches into a round, distributing the stitches evenly. Work 3¼in (8cm) stockinette stitch in rounds, then change color to orange red.

Top | Decrease for the top as follows:
Knit 1, slip 1, knit 1, pass slipped stitch over (see page 134), knit 4, knit 2 together, knit 1. Repeat from * to *.
Knit one round on these 16 stitches.
Next row: *Knit 1, slip 1, knit 1, pass slipped stitch over, knit 2, knit 2 together, knit 1*. Repeat from * to *.
Knit one round on these 12 stitches.
Next row: *Knit 1, slip 1, knit 1, pass slipped stitch over, knit 2 together, knit 1*. Repeat from * to *. (8 stitches remain).
Cut off the yarn, thread the end through all the stitches, pull tight and darn in on the inside.

Thumb | Arrange the 6 stitches from the safety pins with 2 stitches on each of three needles, join into a round and pick up and knit 1 stitch between the last and first stitches of the round, next to the hand.
On these 7 stitches work 3¼in (8cm) stockinette stitch in rounds. On the last round knit 2 together 3 times, knit 1 (4 stitches remain).
Cut off the yarn, thread the end through all the stitches, pull tight and darn in on the inside.

Finishing | Draw the stitches together firmly where the hand joins the thumb. Darn in all the ends. Make the second mitten in the same way.

Pattern

PATTERN DIAGRAM
Measurements in inches (cm)

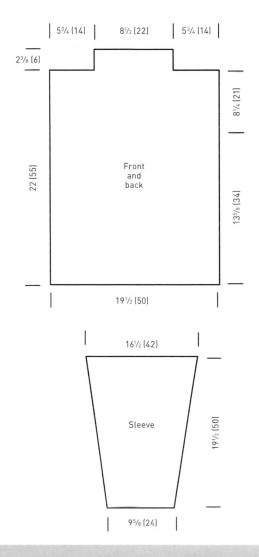

5¾ (14)   8½ (22)   5¾ (14)

2⅜ (6)

8¼ (21)

22 (55)

Front and back

13⅝ (34)

19½ (50)

16½ (42)

Sleeve

19½ (50)

9⅝ (24)

17

Uptown style

OPEN COAT WITH TIE BELT

GAUGE

5.5 stitches and 20 rows in fisherman's rib on US17 (12mm) needles = 4in (10cm) square.

STITCHES

Fisherman's rib | Row 1 (right-side row): Knit 1 (edge stitch), *knit 1, yarn over, slip 1 purlwise*; repeat from * to *, ending with knit 1, knit 1 (edge stitch).
Row 2 (wrong-side row): Knit 1 (edge stitch), * yarn over, slip 1 purlwise, knit 1 stitch together with the yarn over from the previous row*; repeat from * to *, ending with yarn over, slip 1 purlwise, knit 1 (edge stitch).
Row 3: Knit 1, *knit 1 together with the yarn over in the previous row, yarn over, slip 1 purlwise *; repeat from * to * ending with knit 1 together with yarn over in the previous row and 1 edge stitch.
Repeat rows 2 and 3.
Knit as loosely as possible.

Edge stitches | Work the first and last stitches of every row knitwise.

OPEN COAT WITH TIE BELT

Size: S–M

Style: narrow, figure-hugging. A striking pattern that looks especially good on taller figures. Newly knitted, the length is 40in (100cm), but because of the stitch used and the weight of the yarn, it will stretch to as much as 46in (115cm).

MATERIALS

- 11 balls of Classic Elite Toboggan (87yd/100g; 70% merino/30% alpaca) in black
- US17 (12mm) circular needle 40in (100cm) long
- Set of US15 (10mm/UK000) double-pointed needles
- USL-11 (8mm/UK0) crochet hook
- Stitch markers or safety pins
- Stitch holders or spare needles

Pattern

OPEN COAT WITH TIE BELT

PATTERN DIAGRAM
Measurements in inches (cm).

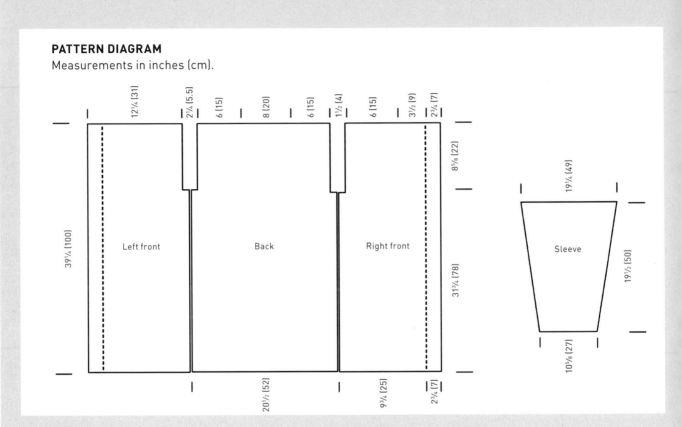

TO MAKE

Back and front | The coat is knitted in one piece in long rows up to the armholes. On a US17 (12mm) circular needle cast on 65 stitches. Knit the 1st row (wrong-side row) as follows: knit 1 (edge stitch), then purl 1, knit 1 alternately, ending with knit 1 (edge stitch).
Continue in fisherman's rib until work measures 31¾in (78cm). Then divide the 65 stitches into the fronts and back as follows:

18 stitches for the right front, 29 stitches for the back and 18 stitches for the left front. Mark the imaginary seams with stitch markers or safety pins.

Back armholes | Finish the back first. Cast off the first 2 stitches of the next two rows. Work a further 8⅝in (22cm) in fisherman's rib on the remaining 25 stitches.

Shoulders and back neck | When work measures 39¼in (100cm), work 8 stitches, cast off the center 9 stitches and work to the end of the row. In the following row, cast off the remaining 8 stitches for the shoulder, then cast off the 8 stitches at the other side.

Front armhole and shoulder | Finish the fronts separately.
At the start of the row (armhole edge), cast off 1 stitch and continue working on the remaining 17 stitches.
When work measures 39¼in (100cm), cast off the first 4 stitches at the neck edge (13 stitches remain).
At the armhole edge, cast off 8 stitches for the shoulder and slip the remaining 5 stitches onto a holder for the collar.

Join the shoulder seams | Turn the coat to the wrong side and sew the shoulders together or graft together on the right side.

Collar | Starting with the left front, with wrong side facing, knit the 5 stitches from the holder, pick up 9 stitches along the back neck and knit the 5 stitches from the holder of the right front (19 stitches).
Continue in fisherman's rib, so that the stitches from the holders continue the pattern correctly.
When the collar measures 4¾in (12cm), cast off all stitches loosely.

Sleeves | Cast on 15 stitches and work a wrong-side row in knit 1 purl 1 rib. Continue in fisherman's rib. Work the first and last stitches of each row as a knit 1 edge stitch.
Increase 1 stitch at each end of every 12th row 6 times (27 stitches).

When work measures 19½in (50cm), cast off all stitches loosely.

Belt | For the belt, work on 2 needles from the set of US15 (10mm) double-pointed needles. Cast on 5 stitches and work in knit 1 purl 1 rib. Continue in rib until the work measures 67in (170cm), then cast off all stitches.

Belt loops | With an L-11 (8mm) crochet hook, on the side seam about 5¼in (13cm) below the armhole, insert the hook into a knit stitch, crochet 8 chain and fasten off with a slip stitch into a knit stitch 3¼in (8cm) below the start of the loop.
Thread the ends through to the inside and darn them in.
Make a second loop on the other side seam.

Making up | Sew in the sleeves. Darn in all the ends.

Instead of the knitted belt, you can wear a narrow leather belt with your long coat instead. Very chic and sleek!

Casual duo

SMOOTH COLOR-BLOCK SWEATER
WITH LONG SCARF

GAUGE

13 stitches and 19 rows in stockinette stitch on
US10½ (7mm/UK2) needles = 4in (10cm) square.

STITCHES

Stockinette stitch | In rows: on right-side rows
knit all stitches, on wrong-side rows purl all
stitches.
In rounds: knit all stitches.
Reverse stockinette stitch | In rows: on right-
side rows purl all stitches, on wrong-side rows
knit all stitches.
In rounds: purl all stitches.

FOR THE SWEATER

Back and front | The sweater is knitted in one
piece in rounds up to the armholes. With US10½
(7mm) circular needle and light red yarn, cast on
120 (128:136) stitches and join into a round.
For the rolled edge, work 3 rounds stockinette
stitch and one round purl, then continue in
stockinette stitch.
Mark the imaginary side seams with stitch
markers or safety pins. The front and back each
consist of 60 (64:68) stitches. The rounds begin at
the right edge of the front.

**SMOOTH COLOR-BLOCK SWEATER
WITH LONG SCARF**
Sizes S, M, L
Measurements for size S are in front
of parentheses: sizes M and L are
inside parentheses (M:L). If only one
measurement is given, it applies
to all sizes.
Style: close-fitting
Scarf: 94½in (240cm) long and 6¾in
(17cm) wide

MATERIALS

- 4 (5:5) balls of Trendsetter Yarns
  Merino 12 (136yd/100g; 100% wool)
  in charcoal and 272 (272:300) yd in
  light wine
- US10½ (7mm/UK2) circular needles
  24 and 32in (60 and 80cm) long
- Set of US10½ (7mm/UK2)
  double-pointed needles
- Stitch holders or spare needles
- Stitch markers or safety pins

Pattern

SMOOTH COLOR-BLOCK SWEATER

PATTERN DIAGRAM
Measurements in inches (cm).

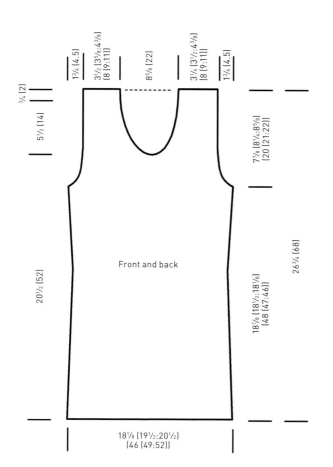

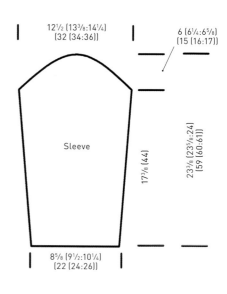

When work measures 6in (15cm), change to dark gray and reverse stockinette stitch, so that the purl stitches can now be seen on the outside (or right side) of the work.

Decrease for waistline | The sweater is slightly shaped. For this, stitches are decreased at both sides.
When the work measures 8¼in (21cm), purl together the second and third stitches and the third-to-last and second-last stitches of the front and back, i.e., decrease a total of 4 stitches in this round.
Repeat these decreases twice more in every following 4th round (108 (116:124) stitches remain).
Work 4 rounds in reverse stockinette stitch then increase to replace the previous decreases by purling into the front and back of the second and second-to-last stitches of the front and back.
Repeat the increases twice more in every following 4th round, until there are once again 120 (128:136) stitches on the needle.

Divide for back and front | When work measures 18⅞ (18½:18⅛)in (48 (47:46)cm), divide for the armholes. The back and front are finished separately and worked in rows.
Divide the stitches into 60 (64:68) stitches each for the front and back. Work the back first.

Armholes | Cast off 3 stitches at the start of the next 2 rows. Then decrease at each side 2 stitches once and 1 stitch once (48 (52:56)

stitches remain on the needle). Continue without further shaping until back measures 26in (66cm).

Back neck | When back measures 26in (66cm), slip the center 18 stitches onto a spare needle or stitch holder.
Finish the right and left sides of the back separately by casting off at the neck edge on every other row 3 stitches once and 2 stitches once.
When back measures 26¾in (68cm), slip the remaining 10 (12:14) stitches onto holders for the shoulders. They will later be knitted together with the shoulder stitches of the front.

Front neck | When front measures 20½in (52cm), slip the center 16 stitches onto a spare needle or a stitch holder. Finish the right and left sides of the front separately by casting off at the neck edge on every other row 2 stitches twice and 1 stitch twice.
When fronts measure 26¾in (68cm), slip the remaining shoulder stitches onto stitch holders, as for the back.

Join the shoulder seams | Turn the sweater to the wrong side and join one shoulder seam by knitting together 1 stitch of the back and 1 stitch of the front shoulder. Next row: cast off all stitches. Join the second shoulder seam in the same way.
Alternatively, the shoulder stitches can be grafted together or cast off and sewn up later.

Neck border | On the set of double-pointed needles, with the right side of the work facing you and starting at the back right shoulder, pick up 5 stitches from the cast-off edge, 18 stitches from the back neck stitch holder, 5 stitches from the cast-off edge at the other side, 14 stitches down the left side of the front neck opening, 6 cast-off stitches, 16 stitches from the holder, 6 cast-off stitches and 14 stitches up the right side of the front neck opening (84 stitches). Work 2 rows stockinette stitch, then cast off all stitches loosely.

Sleeves | The sleeves are knitted in rounds on the set of US10½ (7mm) double-pointed needles. Cast on 28 (31:34) stitches in light red, divide evenly between the needles and work the rolled edge as described for the sweater. Mark the imaginary seam.
After the rolled edge, increase on every 10th round by knitting into the strand between the second and third stitches and between the third-to-last and second-last stitches. Repeat 6 more times, until there are 42 (45:48) stitches on the needles.
When the work measures 10in (25cm), change to dark gray and reverse stockinette stitch.

Sleeve top | When work measures 17³⁄₈in (44cm) change to working in rows. Because of the curve of the top, it is best to begin by continuing to work on two or three of the double-pointed needles. Later, when there are fewer stitches on the needle, one needle will be enough.
Cast off 3 stitches at the beginning of the next two rows (36 (39:42) stitches remain).
Then at each side, cast off 2 stitches once and 1 stitch three times (26 (29:32) stitches remain). Work 3⁵⁄₈ (4:4³⁄₈)in (9 (10:11)cm) without shaping, then cast off at each end of the next 6 rows:

Size S: cast off 1–0–1–2–3–3 stitches. On the next row cast off the remaining 6 stitches.
Size M: cast off 1–1–1–2–3–3 and the remaining 7 stitches on the next row.
Size L: cast off 1–1–1–2–3–4 and the remaining 8 stitches on the next row.

Finishing | Sew in the sleeves. Darn in all the ends. Lightly steam the sweater or let dry under a damp cloth.

FOR THE LONG SCARF

With US10½ (7mm) circular needle and dark gray, cast on 22 stitches and work in stockinette stitch in rows.
Work the first stitch of every row as an edge stitch: on right-side rows slip the stitch knitwise, on wrong-side rows purlwise.
Change color after every 14 rows, knitting broad stripes in light red and dark gray.
When work measures 47in (120cm) after a light red stripe, reduce the width of the stripes and work 2 rows in dark gray and 2 rows in light red alternately. Do not cut off the yarn at the end of the narrow stripes; work it in at the edge.
When work measures 94½in (240cm) after a light red stripe, knit a small rolled edge in dark gray, as described for the sweater on page 23, and cast off all stitches.
Darn in the ends and steam the scarf lightly. It will roll up a little; this effect is deliberate.

City slicker

PONCHO WITH WRIST WARMERS

GAUGE
14 stitches and 20 rows in stockinette stitch on US10 (6mm/UK4) needles = 4in (10cm) square.

STITCHES
Stockinette stitch | In rounds knit all stitches.
Ribbed border | Knit 1 purl 1 alternately.
Zigzag pattern | Work the zigzag pattern from the chart over 16 stitches. The figures to the right of the chart refer to the pattern rounds. On the even-numbered rounds in between, knit all stitches. Keep repeating rounds 1–28.

FOR THE PONCHO
The poncho is knitted in one piece in rounds from the top down. It starts at the roll collar with a ribbed border and finishes at the hem, also with a small ribbed border. The rounds start between the left arm and the back. Mark the beginning of the round with a stitch marker or safety pin. When you reach the appropriate number of stitches, change to the next-longest needle.

Roll collar | With the set of double-pointed needles, cast on 76 stitches and work 6in (15cm) in knit 1 purl 1 rib. In the next round, change to stockinette stitch and increase 14 stitches, evenly distributed (90 stitches).

Divide the stitches | Divide the stitches into four areas: 29 stitches for the back, 16 stitches for the right arm, 29 stitches for the front, and 16 stitches for the left arm. To make it easier to keep track, mark the four areas with stitch markers. Work the zigzag pattern according to the chart on page 31, over the center 16 stitches of the front.

PONCHO WITH WRIST WARMERS
One size
Style: generous, but not full

MATERIALS
- 6 balls Trendsetter Yarns Merino 12 (136yd/100g; 100% merino wool) in light pearl for the poncho and 136yd for the wrist warmers
- US10 (6mm/UK4) circular needles, 24 and 32in (60 and 80cm) long
- Set of US10 (6mm/UK4) double-pointed needles
- Stitch markers or safety pins
- Stitch holders or cable needles

Increases | After two rounds, begin increasing. Work the increases with a yarn over before and after each of the 16 sleeve stitches. Increase 4 stitches per round, 5 times in successive rounds (90 + 20 = 110 stitches) and 8 times in every other round (110 + 32 = 142 stitches). Then increase 5 times in every 5th round, so that when you reach the arm openings, there are 162 stitches in total on the needle.

Arm openings | When work measures 17¾in (45cm), start the arm openings. At this point you will have 65 stitches for the back, 16 stitches for the right arm, 65 stitches for the front, and 16 stitches for the left arm.
The arm openings will be positioned on either side of the center 51 stitches of the front, with 7 stitches to the right and left of them. Work one more round without any increases, ending this round at 7 stitches before the end of the front section, ready to start the arm openings.
Work in rows, starting at the left arm opening with a right-side row: knit 7 stitches to the right of the opening, 16 stitches of the left sleeve, 65 stitches across the back, 16 stitches of the right sleeve and 7 stitches to the left of the other opening.
Turn and work the wrong-side row.
Slip the center front 51 stitches onto a holder. Work 10in (25cm), remembering to increase either side of the sleeves as before, and continue increasing in every 5th row (another 10 × 4 stitches = 40 stitches; total stitch count = 202).
Slip the stitches onto a spare needle and work 10in (25cm) on the 51 stitches between the openings, including the zigzag pattern.
Now return all the stitches to the circular needle and work in rounds. Continue without further increasing until the work measures 27½in (70cm).

Bottom border | Work 4in (10cm) in rib, then cast off all stitches loosely.

Arm opening borders | With the circular needle, pick up 45 stitches along one edge of the opening and work ¾in (2cm) in rib, starting and ending with a knit stitch. Cast off all stitches. Work the other 3 borders in the same way.
Sew the narrow edges of the borders to the fronts, with the top layer pointing toward the side and the lower layer toward the center of the garment.

Finishing | Darn in all the ends.

FOR THE WRIST WARMERS
On the set of US10 (6mm) double-pointed needles, cast on 28 stitches and distribute evenly between the needles. Work 2in (5cm) in knit 1 purl 1 rib.
For the thumb opening, change to working in rows. Knit into the front and back of the last stitch of the last needle, so that the rows begin and end with a knit stitch.
Work 2⅜in (6cm) (total length 4⅜in (11cm)), then cast off the extra stitch and change back to working in rounds.
When work measures 8¾in (22cm) and again at 11¼in (28cm), increase by working make 1 in the strands before and after the 6th stitch for the right wrist warmer and before and after the 22nd stitch for the left wrist warmer (32 stitches).
When work measures 13⅝in (34cm), cast off all stitches loosely and sew in the ends.

Chart and pattern

PONCHO WITH WRIST WARMERS

CHART
Zigzag pattern

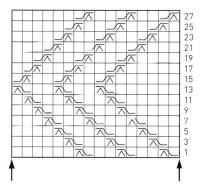

Key:

 = Knit 1

= Twist 2 right: slip 1 stitch onto a cable needle and hold at back of work, slip the next stitch purlwise with the yarn behind the stitch, then knit the stitch from the cable needle.

= Twist 2 left: slip 1 stitch onto a cable needle and hold at front of work, knit the next stitch, then slip the stitch from the cable needle purlwise with the yarn behind the stitch.

PATTERN DIAGRAM
Measurements in inches (cm)

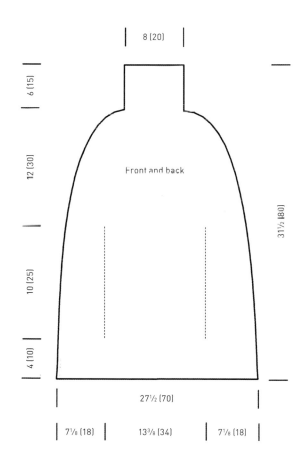

8 (20)

6 (15)

12 (30)

Front and back

31½ (80)

10 (25)

4 (10)

27½ (70)

7⅛ (18) 13⅜ (34) 7⅛ (18)

All wrapped up

CASUAL WRAP

GAUGE
8 stitches and 12 rows in stockinette stitch
on US15 (10mm/UK000) needles = 4in
(10cm) square.

STITCHES
Small basketweave pattern | Work the small
basketweave pattern from the chart on page 34
over multiples of 6 stitches + 2.
The figures to the right of the chart refer to the
right-side rows, those to the left the wrong-side
rows. Begin with the stitches before the first
arrow, continue repeating the pattern (6 stitches)
between the arrows and finish with the stitches
after the second arrow. For clarity, three pattern
repeats are shown. Work from the bottom of the
chart up and keep repeating rows 1–12.
Rib border | knit 1 purl 1 alternately.

TO MAKE
The wrap is knitted in a single piece, beginning at
the back hem and ending at the front hem.

Back | On a US15 (10mm) circular needle, cast on
86 stitches and work 2in (5cm) in knit 1 purl 1 rib.
Then work from the chart and keep repeating
rows 1–12.

Start the round with 2 stitches for the start of the
pattern, then work 14 repeats of the 6 stitches
between the arrows.

Neck opening | When work measures
approximately 30in (75cm), after an 8th row of
the chart, cast off the center 10 stitches.

Fronts | Finish the right and left fronts
separately. Leave the stitches for the left front

CASUAL WRAP
One size
Style: generous

MATERIALS
• 10 hanks of Classic Elite Toboggan
  (87yd/50g; 70% merino/30%
  alpaca) in black
• US15 (10mm/UK000) circular
  needle, 40in (100cm) long
• Circular needle to hold the stitches
  for the front

on a stitch holder and start with the right front. Continue the chart pattern as started on the back and work over 6 repeats plus 2 stitches for the pattern at the start of the row. When work measures 58in (145cm), finish with

2in (5cm) in knit 1 purl 1 rib.
Work the left front in the same way.

Finishing | Darn in all the ends.

Chart and pattern

CASUAL WRAP

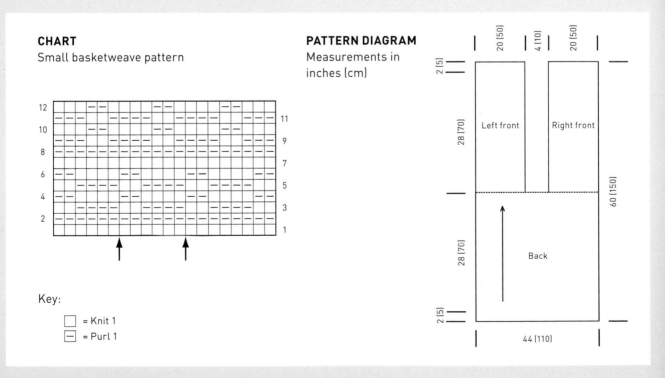

CHART
Small basketweave pattern

Key:

☐ = Knit 1
⊟ = Purl 1

PATTERN DIAGRAM
Measurements in inches (cm)

Left front

Right front

Back

20 (50)   4 (10)   20 (50)

2 (5)

28 (70)

60 (150)

28 (70)

2 (5)

44 (110)

Urban chic

COZY TOP WITH MATCHING COWL

GAUGE
9 stitches and 12 rows in stockinette stitch
on US15 (10mm/UK000) needles = 4in
(10cm) square.

STITCHES
Stockinette stitch | In rows: right-side rows knit
all stitches, wrong-side rows purl all stitches.
In rounds: knit all stitches.
Reverse stockinette stitch | In rows: right-side
rows purl all stitches, wrong-side rows knit all
stitches. In rounds: purl all stitches.
Rib borders | Knit 2 purl 2 alternately.

FOR THE TOP
The top is worked in rounds up to the armholes.

Rib border | With US15 (10mm) circular needle
cast on 80 (88:96) stitches, join into a round and
work 3¼in (8cm) in knit 2 purl 2 rib.

Front and back | Change to stockinette stitch,
increasing 8 stitches evenly distributed in the
first round (88 (96:104) stitches).
Mark the imaginary side seams with stitch
markers or safety pins.

COZY TOP WITH MATCHING COWL
Sizes S, M, L
Measurements for size S are in front
of parentheses; sizes M and L are
inside parentheses (M:L). If only one
measurement is given, it applies
to all sizes.
Style: generous
Cowl: 32in (80cm) circumference
and 16in (40cm) wide

MATERIALS
- 10 (12:14) balls Lana Grossa
  Ragazza Lei Mouline (44yd/50g;
  100% wool) in anthracite marl
  (col. 662) for top and 4 balls for
  cowl
- US15 (10mm/UK000) circular
  needles, 24 and 32in (60 and 80cm)
  long
- Set of US15 (10mm/UK000)
  double-pointed needles
- Stitch markers or safety pins
- Stitch holder or spare needle
- Tapestry needle for finishing

The front and back each have 44 (48:52) stitches. The rounds start at the right front edge.

Increasing at both sides | The top has very wide shoulders; increases are worked at both sides. In every 4th round make 1 four times by working into the strands between the first and second stitches and the second-to-last and last stitches of the front and back, i.e., 4 stitches added in every increase round. Work these increases 9 (10:11) times. When all increases have been worked, there will be 62 (68:74) stitches each for the front and back, i.e., 124 (136:148) stitches in total on the needle.

Pattern stripe on front | When work measures 11 (11⅞:12½)in (28 (30:32)cm), on the front work 4in (10cm) in reverse stockinette stitch for the front stripe, then change back to stockinette stitch.

Divide for back and front | When work measures 12½ (13½:14¼)in (32 (34:36)cm) divide for the armholes and finish the back and front separately (62 (68:74) stitches each). Finish the back first, by working a further 8in (20cm) in stockinette stitch in rows without shaping.

Back shoulder slope | Since the shoulders are extra-wide, a small slope is worked. When work measures 20½ (21¼:22)in (52 (54:56)cm), decrease at the start (outer edge) for two rows each in the following sequence: for size S decrease 2–2–3–3–5–6 stitches, for size M 2–2–4–4–6–6 stitches and for size L 2–3–4–5–6–7 stitches. Slip the remaining 20 stitches onto a spare needle for the back neck.

Front neck | When work measures 19 (19¾:20½)in (48 (50:52)cm), slip the center 14 stitches onto a spare needle or a stitch holder.
Finish the right and left fronts separately. In every other row, cast off at the neck edge 2 stitches once and 1 stitch once.
Continue without further shaping until work measures 20½ (21¼:22)in (52 (54:56)cm), then work the shoulder decreases as described for the back.

Join shoulder seams | Join the shoulder seams with a tapestry needle, either by sewing with the wrong sides together or by grafting from the right side.

Neck border | With the set of double-pointed needles, pick up the 20 stitches of the back neck from the holder, 18 stitches down one side of the front neck opening, 20 stitches of the front neck (14 from the stitch holder plus the cast-off

The neck border is designed not to lie flat but to form a small stand-up collar. If you would prefer a flat border, pick up only 60 stitches instead of 76 when you work the neck border.

Pattern

PATTERN DIAGRAM
Measurements in inches (cm)

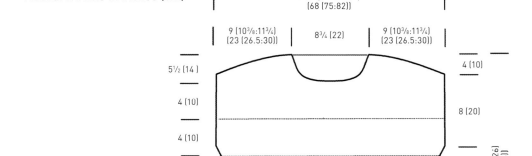

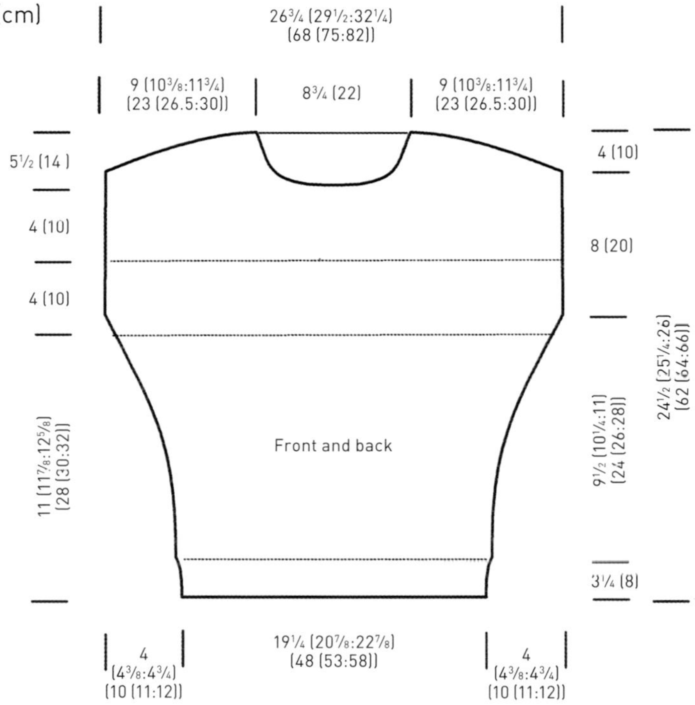

26¾ (29½:32¼)
(68 (75:82))

9 (10⅜:11¾)
(23 (26.5:30))

8¾ (22)

9 (10⅜:11¾)
(23 (26.5:30))

5½ (14)

4 (10)

4 (10)

4 (10)

8 (20)

24½ (25¼:26)
(62 (64:66))

11 (11⅞:12⅝)
(28 (30:32))

9½ (10¼:11)
(24 (26:28))

Front and back

3¼ (8)

4
(4⅜:4¾)
(10 (11:12))

19¼ (20⅞:22⅞)
(48 (53:58))

4
(4⅜:4¾)
(10 (11:12))

stitches on either side) and 18 stitches up the other side of the front neck opening (76 stitches). Work 1¼in (3cm) in knit 1 purl 1 rib in rounds, then cast off all stitches loosely.

Sleeve border | With the set of double-pointed needles, pick up 44 stitches around the armhole and work 1¼in (3cm) in knit 1 purl 1 rib in rounds, then cast off all stitches loosely.

FOR THE COWL
With US15 (10mm) circular needle, cast on 72 stitches and join into a round. Work 15¾in (40cm) in knit 2 purl 2 rib in rounds, then cast off all stitches loosely.

Finishing | Darn in all the ends.

Streetwise cool

LONG BLOCK-STRIPE CARDIGAN

GAUGE
11 stitches and 16 rows in stockinette stitch on US10½ (7mm/UK2) needles = 4in (10cm) square.

STITCHES
Stockinette stitch | In rows: right-side rows knit all stitches, wrong-side rows purl all stitches. In rounds: knit all stitches.
Reverse stockinette stitch | In rows: right-side rows purl all stitches, wrong-side rows knit all stitches.
In rounds: purl all stitches.
Rib borders | Knit 1 purl 1 alternately.

TO MAKE
Pockets | Start by knitting the pockets. They will be worked into the fronts of the cardigan later. Cast on 17 stitches in oatmeal and work 5¼in (13cm) in stockinette stitch. When the pocket measures 5¼in (13cm), cast off the first two and last two stitches of the last right-side row. Slip the remaining 13 stitches onto a holder. Make the second pocket in the same way.

Back and front | The cardigan is knitted in one piece in rows as far as the armholes. With US10½ (7mm) circular needle and dark gray marl, cast on 99 (111:123) stitches and work in knit 1 purl 1 rib. Start with a wrong-side row and purl 2 stitches, then knit 1 purl 1 alternately and end with purl 2.

LONG BLOCK-STRIPE CARDIGAN
Measurements for size S are in front of parentheses: sizes M and L are inside parentheses (M:L). If only one measurement is given, it applies to all sizes.
Style: semi-fitted; narrow, but not constricting

MATERIALS
- 2 balls of Lana Grossa Yak Merino (120yd/50g) in curry marl (col. 1), 5 (6:7) balls in oatmeal (col. 10) and 6 (7:8) balls in dark gray marl (col. 11)
- US10½ (7mm/UK2) circular needles 24 and 32in (60 and 80cm) long
- Set of US10½ (7mm/UK2) double-pointed needles
- Stitch markers or safety pins
- Stitch holders or spare needles
- 4 buttons, 1in (25mm) diameter

In the following rows work the stitches as they appear.

Work 3¼in (8cm) in rib.

Then change to curry marl and work 6in (15cm) in stockinette stitch. Increase 1 stitch in the first stockinette stitch row by knitting front and back into the 24th (27th:30th) stitch.

Divide the stitches as follows: 24 (27:30) stitches for the right front, 52 (58:64) stitches for the back and 24 (27:30) stitches for the left front. Mark the imaginary side seams with stitch markers or safety pins.

Note | The ribbed front border of the cardigan will be knitted on later and is 1½in (4cm) wide. (This is why the fronts added together have fewer stitches than the back.)

Pockets | When work measures 9in (23cm), change to dark gray marl and in the first dark gray row knit in the pockets as follows:

Knit 5 (6:7) stitches, slip the next 13 stitches onto a holder and knit the 13 stitches of the pocket from the holder, then knit the remaining 6 (8:10) stitches of the right front, the 52 (58:64) stitches of the back and 6 (8:10) stitches of the left front, slip the next 13 stitches onto a holder and knit the 13 stitches of the second pocket from their holder and finish the row by knitting the remaining 5 (6:7) stitches of the left front.

The pocket borders will later be knitted on the stitches from the holders.

Continue in stockinette stitch, changing between oatmeal and dark gray every 3¼in (8cm).

Decrease for the waist at both sides | The cardigan is slightly shaped. Decreases for this are worked at both sides.

When work measures 17¾ (17:16¼)in (45 (43:41)cm), knit together the third-to-last and second-to-last stitches of the right front (i.e., the 22nd and 23rd stitches for size S, the 25th and 26th stitches for size M and the 28th and 29th stitches for size L), the 2nd and 3rd stitches of the back, the third-to-last and second-to-last stitches of the back and the 2nd and 3rd stitches of the left front. 4 stitches are decreased in each decrease row.

Repeat the decreases twice more on every 8th row (88 (100:112)) stitches.

Work 7 rows and then start increasing again by knitting in the front and back of the 2nd stitch before and the 2nd stitch after the side seams. Repeat the increases twice more in every 8th row, until there are once again 100 (112:124) stitches on the needle.

Front neck slope | When work measures 24¾in (63cm), begin decreasing for the neck slope on both fronts and continue until only the 12 (14:16) stitches for the shoulders remain.

On the right front, decrease by working the third and fourth stitches as slip 1 knit 1 pass slipped stitch over, and on the left front by knitting together the fourth-to-last and third-to-last stitches.

For size S: decrease on every 3rd right-side row. For sizes M and L: decrease in every 2nd and 3rd right-side row alternately.

Do not forget to start working the armholes when the work reaches 29½ (28¾:28)in (75 (73:71)cm) in length.

Divide for fronts and back | When work measures 29½ (28¾:28)in (75 (73:71)cm), begin casting off for the armholes and finish the back and fronts separately. Continue decreasing at the front neck edge as described above. The center 52 (58:64) stitches form the back, and the remaining stitches make up the right and left fronts. The number of stitches for the fronts may vary, depending on how many decreases have been worked.

Back armhole | Finish the back first. At the beginning of the next 6 rows, cast off 2 stitches four times and 1 stitch twice (42 (48:54) stitches remain). Continue working in stripe sequence.

Back neck | When work measures 37in (94cm), cast off the center 18 (20:22) stitches. On each side work 2 rows stockinette stitch then slip the remaining 12 (14:16) stitches onto holders.

Pattern

LUNG BLOCK-STRIPE CARDIGAN

PATTERN DIAGRAM
Measurements in inches (cm)

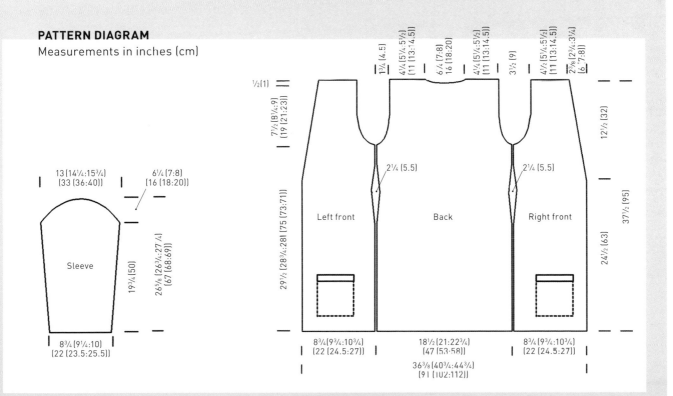

Front armholes | Work the armhole decreases as for the back, while continuing to decrease at the neck edge as before.

When work measures 37½in (95cm), slip the remaining 12 (14:16) stitches onto holders for the shoulders. They will later be knitted together with the shoulder stitches of the back.

Join the shoulder seams | Turn the cardigan to the wrong side and knit the shoulder stitches together by knitting 1 stitch of the back together with 1 stitch of the front each time. In the next row, cast off all stitches. Join the second shoulder in the same way.

Pockets | With dark gray yarn, pick up and knit the 13 stitches for the pocket border from the holder. Work 1⅝in (4cm) in rib. Then cast off all stitches. Sew the side edges invisibly to the fronts.

On the wrong side, sew the pockets to the fronts with whip stitch, so that the seam does not show on the right side of the garment.

Buttonhole and button band | With dark gray marl yarn, pick up stitches evenly along the front edges and back neck. Work ¾in (2cm) in rib, beginning and ending at the hem edges with purl 1. On the next right-side row, 6¾in (17cm) from the hem of the right front, cast off 2 stitches for the first buttonhole. Make 3 more buttonholes in the same way, with 6in (15cm) between them. In the following wrong-side row, cast on 2 stitches over each buttonhole. When the band is 1⅝in (4cm) wide, cast off all stitches.

Sleeves | The sleeves are knitted in rounds on double-pointed needles, and have no seam. With dark gray marl and a set of US10½ (7mm) double-pointed needles, cast on 24 (26:28)

stitches and distribute the stitches evenly. Mark the imaginary seam.

Work 2⅜in (6cm) in knit 1 purl 1 rib.

Change to stockinette stitch and work 4¾in (12cm) in curry marl.

Then continue in alternate 3¼in (8cm) stripes of oatmeal and dark gray.

Increase a total of 12 (14:16) stitches by knitting into the strand between the second and third stitches and between the third-to-last and second-to-last stitches of the round: for size S, in every 10th round 6 times; for size M, in every 8th round 7 times; for size L, in every 7th round 8 times; (36 (40:44) stitches on needles).

Sleeve top | When sleeve measures 19½in (50cm), change to working in rows, at first with two or three needles from the set. Later, one needle will be enough.

Cast off 2 stitches at the beginning of the next 4 rows and 1 stitch at the beginning of the following 2 rows (26 (30:34) stitches remain). Cast off 1 stitch at each end of every 4th row 3 times (20 (24:28) stitches remain).

When sleeve top measures 4⅜ (5:6)in (11 (13:15)cm) from the start of the decreases, cast off at each side as follows:

For size S: for two rows each in the following sequence: cast off 1–1–2–3 stitches (14 stitches in total). Cast off the remaining 6 stitches in the next right-side row.

For size M: for two rows each in the following sequence: cast off 1–2–3–3 stitches (18 stitches in total). Cast off the remaining 6 stitches.

For size L: for two rows each in the following sequence: cast off 2–2–3–4 (22 stitches in total). Cast off the remaining 6 stitches.

Finishing | Sew in the sleeves. Darn in all the ends.

45

Country style

ESCAPE TO THE COUNTRY, WHERE THE FRESH BREEZE WILL BLOW THOSE COBWEBS AWAY—AND IF THERE'S A NIP IN THE AIR, A CHUNKY KNIT WILL KEEP YOU COMFY AND COZY

Rustic charm

HOODED JACKET WITH TOGGLES

GAUGE
10 stitches and 15 rows in stockinette stitch on US13 (9mm/UK00) needles = 4in (10cm) square.

STITCHES
Stockinette stitch | In rows: right-side rows knit all stitches, wrong-side rows purl all stitches. In rounds: knit all stitches.
Reverse stockinette stitch | In rows: right-side rows purl all stitches, wrong-side rows knit all stitches.
In rounds: purl all stitches.
Rib borders | Knit 1 purl 1 alternately.
Cable pattern for sizes S and M | Work from the chart on page 51. Work the 17 (19) stitch repeat between the arrows 5 times, ending with 18 stitches after the 2nd arrow (103 (113)) stitches. The figures to the right refer to the right-side rows; in the wrong-side rows, work the stitches as they appear. Work rows 1–63 once.
Cable pattern for size L | Work the 18 stitches between the arrows according to the chart on page 52. The figures to the right refer to the right-side rows; in the wrong-side rows, work the stitches as they appear. Work rows 1–63 once.

HOODED JACKET WITH TOGGLES
Sizes S, M, L
Measurements for size S are in front of parentheses: sizes M and L are inside parentheses (M:L). If only one measurement is given, it applies to all sizes.
Style: semi-fitted; narrow, but not constricting

MATERIALS
- 10 (11:12) balls Lion Brand Wool-Ease Thick and Quick (106yd/170g; 80% acrylic, 20% wool) in Lemongrass
- US13 (9mm/UK00) circular needles, 24 and 32in (60 and 80cm) long
- Set of US13 (9mm/UK00) double-pointed needles
- US10/J (6mm/UK4) crochet hook
- Stitch markers or safety pins
- Stitch holder and cable needle
- 2 horn toggles

TO MAKE

Back and front | The jacket is knitted in one piece in long rows up to the armholes.

Rib border | On a US13 (9mm) circular needle, cast on 93 (103:115) stitches and work 3¼in (8cm) in knit 1 purl 1 rib. Start with a wrong-side row, beginning and ending with 1 purl.
When work measures 3¼in (8cm), increase 24 (24:25) stitches evenly in a wrong-side row (117 (127:140) stitches).

Positioning the cable pattern | Allocate the stitches as follows:
7 stitches for the ribbed front border, 24 (27:30) stitches for the right front, 55 (59:66) stitches for the back, 24 (27:30) stitches for the left front, 7 stitches for the ribbed front border.
Number of repeats:
For size S: 6 repeats (5 repeats of 17 stitches and 1 of 18 stitches) = 103 stitches.
For size M: 6 repeats (5 repeats of 19 stitches and 1 of 18 stitches) = 113 stitches.
For size L: 7 repeats of 18 stitches = 126 stitches.
Mark the imaginary side seams with stitch markers or safety pins.
Work the cable pattern from the chart until the work measures 17⅜in (44cm) on row 59.

Rib pattern for the waist | In row 59, the cables are reduced from 6 stitches to 4, according to the chart (12 (12:14) stitches fewer).
At the same time, the 4 purl stitches before and after the cables are each reduced to 3 stitches, by working purl 2 together (12 (12:14) stitches fewer).
Work 6⅜in (16cm) on these 93 (103:112) stitches, working the stitches as they appear. Then work in stockinette stitch, with only the first 7 and last 7 stitches in rib for the border.

Equalize the stitch numbers | To keep the garment symmetrical, increase 1 stitch in the right front and 0 (0:1) stitch in the left front in the first stockinette stitch row (94 (104:114) stitches)

Divide for fronts and back | When work measures 27½ (26¾:26)in (70 (68:66)cm), divide for the armholes and finish the fronts and back separately. The center 44 (48:52) stitches form the back, with 25 (28:31) stitches for each front (94 (104:114) stitches).

Back armhole | Finish the back first. At the start of the following 4 rows, work 2 rows of each of the following; cast off 2 stitches once and 1 stitch once (38 (42:46) stitches). Continue in stockinette stitch without further shaping until the work measures 35½in (90cm).

Back neck | Slip the center 18 stitches onto a holder for the hood and the 10 (12:14) stitches at each side onto separate holders for the shoulders. They will later be knitted together with the shoulder stitches of the fronts.

Front armholes | Finish the fronts separately (25 (28:31) stitches for each). Work the armholes as for the back (22 (25:28) stitches).

Front neck | On both fronts, when the work measures 29½in (75cm), slip the 7 stitches of the border onto a stitch holder and work the neck edge on the remaining 15 (18:21) stitches.
At the neck edge of the following right-side rows, slip 2 stitches 1 (2:2) times and 1 stitch 3 (2:3) times onto safety pins. Continue in stockinette stitch on the remaining 10 (12:14) stitches.
When work measures 35½in (90cm), slip these stitches onto holders for the shoulders.

Charts

HOODED JACKET WITH TOGGLES

CHART

Cable pattern for size S

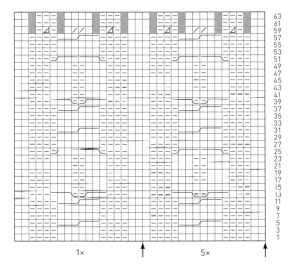

CHART

Cable pattern for size M

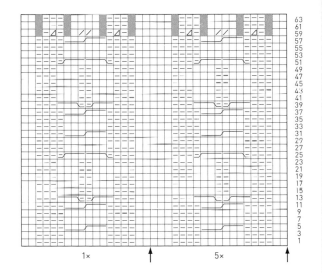

Key:

☐ = Knit 1

⊟ = Purl 1

◩ = Knit 2 together

◪ = Purl 2 together

▨ = No stitch. Ignore when knitting

= Cross 4 right: Slip 1 stitch onto a cable needle and leave at back of work; knit 3, then purl the stitch from the cable needle

= Cross 4 left: Slip 3 stitches onto a cable needle and leave at front of work; purl 1, then knit the 3 stitches from the cable needle

= Cross 6 right: Slip 3 stitches onto a cable needle and leave at back of work; knit 3, then knit the 3 stitches from the cable needle

Chart

CHART
Cable pattern for size L

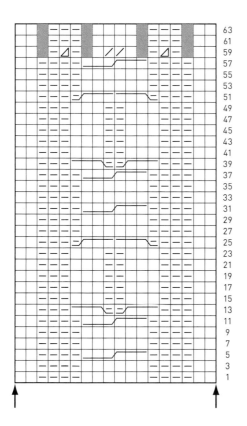

Key: see page 51

Join the shoulder seams | Turn the jacket to the wrong side and join one shoulder seam by knitting together 1 stitch of the back and 1 stitch of the front shoulder. Cast off the stitches one by one. Join the second shoulder seam in the same way. Alternatively, the shoulder stitches can be grafted together or cast off and sewn up later.

Hood | For the hood, with the circular needle pick up the stitches as follows: pick up 7 stitches of the right border, 5 (6:7) stitches from the safety pins of the right neck edge, knit up 5 stitches along the side of the right neck, knit the 18 stitches of the back neck edge from the holder, knit up 5 stitches along the side of the left neck, slip 5 (6:7) stitches from the safety pins of the left neck edge, and 7 stitches of the left border (52 (54:56) stitches).
Continue in rows, working the border stitches in rib and the stitches in between in stockinette stitch.
In the second right-side row after picking up the stitches, decrease 2 stitches evenly distributed for size M and 4 stitches for size L by knitting 2 together (52 stitches on needle for all sizes).
When hood measures 2¾in (7cm), after the 22nd stitch and before the 34th stitch, make 1 by knitting into the loop between stitches. Repeat these increases twice more in every 3rd row (58 stitches).

Shortened rows at top of head | Begin knitting shorter rows. Divide the stitches into 22 for the right side, 14 stitches center strip and 22 for the left side. The 15 stitches to the right and left of the center strip will gradually be decreased into the stitches of the border.
Rib the 7 stitches of the border, knit 15, knit 13 stitches of the center strip, *slip 1, knit 1 (from the side panel), pass slipped stitch over. Turn.

Slip the 1st stitch of the center strip purlwise, purl 12, purl the last stitch of the center strip together with the next stitch (from the side panel). Turn. Slip the 1st stitch knitwise, knit 12 *. Repeat from * to * until only the 7 stitches of the rib border remain on each side. Slip the center 14 stitches onto a spare needle.

Continue the borders | Continue the right border on one needle, knitting the stitch at the end of the row together with the 1st stitch of the center strip from the spare needle. Repeat 7 times in all. Continue the left border in the same way. When the borders meet in the middle, all the stitches of the center strip will have been "used up." Cast off the borders and sew the ends together.

Sleeves | The sleeves are knitted in rounds on the set of US13 (9mm) double-pointed needles, and have no seam.
Cast on 20 (22:24) stitches and distribute evenly between the needles. Mark the imaginary seam. Work 3¼in (8cm) in knit 1 purl 1 rib.
Change to stockinette stitch. Knit 1 round. In the next round, begin increasing by knitting into the strands between the second and third stitches and between the third-to-last and second-to-last stitches of the round, i.e., 2 stitches per round. Continue increasing in this way in every 6th round until there are 34 (36:40) stitches on the needles.

Sleeve tops | When sleeve measures 18⅛in (46cm), change to working in rows, to begin with on two or three needles from the set of double-pointed needles. Later, when fewer stitches remain, one needle will be enough.
At the start of the following 4 rows, work 2 rows each as follows; cast off 2 stitches once and 1

stitch once (28 (30:34) stitches remain). Continue decreasing 1 stitch at each end of every 4th row until 24 (26:30) stitches remain. When work measures 4⅜ (5¼:5½)in (11 (13:14)cm) from the start of the decreases for the top, at the beginning of the following 8 rows, work 2 rows of each of the following; cast off 1–2–2–4 stitches for size S; 1–2–3–4 stitches for size M; and 1–2–3–5 stitches for size L. On the next right-side row, cast off the remaining 6 (6:8) stitches.

Fastening | For the toggle loops, with double yarn and a US10/J (6mm) crochet hook, make a chain 4¾in (12cm) long and fasten off the yarn. Form the chain into a U-shape. Sew 1¼in (3cm) together at the edges to make a loop 1¼in (3cm) long. The seam should be on the underside and will not be visible on the right side. Position the loop on the right-front border, about 19¾in (50cm) from the hem, with the loop extending ¾–1¼in (2–3cm) beyond the border so that the toggle can easily be inserted through it, and sew on with single yarn. Make the second loop in the same way and sew on about 6in (15cm) higher up. Sew the toggles to the left border, opposite the loops.

Finishing | Sew in the sleeves. Darn in all the ends.

Pattern

PATTERN DIAGRAM

Measurements in inches (cm)

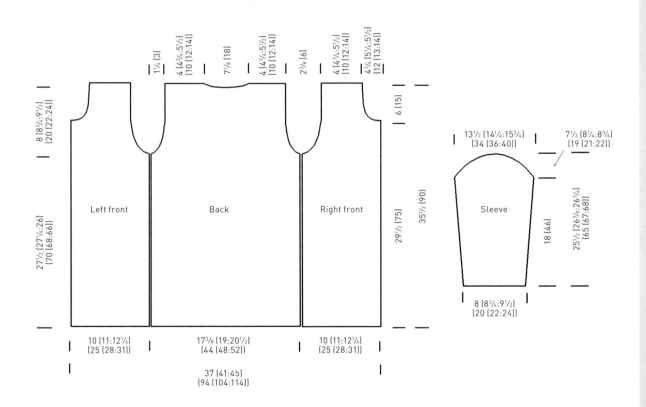

Spring break

LONG TOP WITH COWL, WRIST WARMERS, AND HAT

GAUGE
11 stitches and 16 rows in stockinette stitch on US10½ (7mm/UK2) needles = 4in (10cm) square.

STITCHES
Stockinette stitch | In rows: right-side rows knit all stitches, wrong-side rows purl all stitches.
In rounds: knit all stitches.
Reverse stockinette stitch | In rows: right-side rows purl all stitches, wrong-side rows knit all stitches.
In rounds: purl all stitches.
Garter stitch borders | In rows: knit all stitches.
In rounds: 1 round knit and 1 round purl alternately.

FOR THE TOP
The top is knitted in rounds up to the armholes. With a US10½ (7mm) circular needle, cast on 112 (122:132) stitches, join into a round and work 1⅝in (4cm) in garter stitch.
Change to stockinette stitch and reverse stockinette stitch.

Stitch allocation for front and back |
Front and back each consist of 5 bands of 11 (12:13) stitches, worked alternately in stockinette stitch and reverse stockinette stitch, starting and ending with knit stitches on the right side of work.

LONG TOP WITH COWL, WRIST WARMERS, AND HAT
Sizes S, M, L
Measurements for size S are in front of parentheses: sizes M and L are inside parentheses (M:L). If only one measurement is given, it applies to all sizes.
Style: generous
Cowl: 60in (152cm) circumference and 13¾in (35cm) wide
Hat: to fit head size 21–22½in (53–57cm)

MATERIALS
- 6 (7:7) balls of Lana Grossa Yak Merino (120yd/50g; 30% Merino, 28% alpaca, 22% nylon, 20% yak) in fuchsia marl (col. 005) for top, 3 balls for cowl, 2 balls for hat, and 1 ball for wrist warmers
- US10½ (7mm/UK2) circular needle, 31½in (80cm) long
- US10 (6mm/UK4) and US13 (9mm/UK00) double-pointed needles
- Stitch holder or spare needle

Work 1 purl between the stitches of the front and back on each side to mark the side seams. Rounds begin at the right edge of the front. Stitch allocation: 55 (60:65) stitches for the front in bands, purl 1, 55 (60:65) stitches for the back in bands, purl 1.

Kangaroo pocket | When work measures 6in (15cm), on the front after the 15th (17th:20th) stitch of the round, make 1 by knitting into the strand between this stitch and the next stitch. Continue along the round, making 1 from the strand between each stitch 24 more times, then finish the round without further increases. In the next round, slip the 25 stitches just made onto a spare needle or stitch holder and leave at back of work and slip the original stitches onto a needle from a set of double-pointed needles at front of work. Working on these 25 stitches, finish the pocket first. Work 26 rows, keeping the band pattern the same as before. On every 8th row, purl together the first two stitches and the last two stitches three times (19 stitches remain). After 26 rows, slip these stitches onto a holder. Return to the top and work 26 rounds. In round 27, knit 1 stitch of the pocket and 1 stitch of the top together—knit or purl, depending on the band pattern for each stitch of the pocket, and continue working in rounds on 112 (122:132) stitches.

Increase for the wide sleeves | When work measures 12⅝in (32cm), begin increasing for the sleeves, working the added stitches in the panel pattern, i.e., in reverse stockinette stitch. On front and back, on every 4th row/round, before and after the purl stitch marking the side seam, make 1 stitch by picking up and purling into the loop between the stitches, thus adding 4 stitches per round.

Repeat these increases 10 more times and then 0 (1:2) times on every 2nd row/round (156 (170:184) stitches on the needle).

Divide for front and back | When work measures 23in (58cm), change to working in rows and finish the back first.
Purl the stitches marking the side seams together with the neighboring stitches, giving (77 (84:91) stitches) for the back, and change to working in rows.
Slip the 77 (84:91) stitches for the front onto a spare needle.

Back neck | Continue without shaping until back measures 31½in (80cm). On the next row, cast off the center 17 (18:19) stitches for the back neck. Slip the remaining 30 (33:36) stitches on each side onto holders for the shoulders. They will later be knitted together with the shoulder stitches of the fronts.

Front neck | Return to the front and work as for the back until the front measures 28¼in (72cm). Cast off the center 9 (10:11) stitches for the neck. Finish the right and left sides separately, casting off at the neck edge on every other row 2 stitches once and 1 stitch twice. When work measures 31½in (80cm), slip the remaining 30 (33:36) stitches onto holders. Knit the stitches of the front and back shoulders together on the wrong side. In the next row, cast off all stitches.

Neck border | With the set of 10½in (7mm) double-pointed needles, pick up 60 stitches around the neck edge and work 1⅝in (4cm) garter stitch in rounds. Cast off all stitches loosely.

Pattern

LONG TOP

PATTERN DIAGRAM
Measurements in inches (cm)

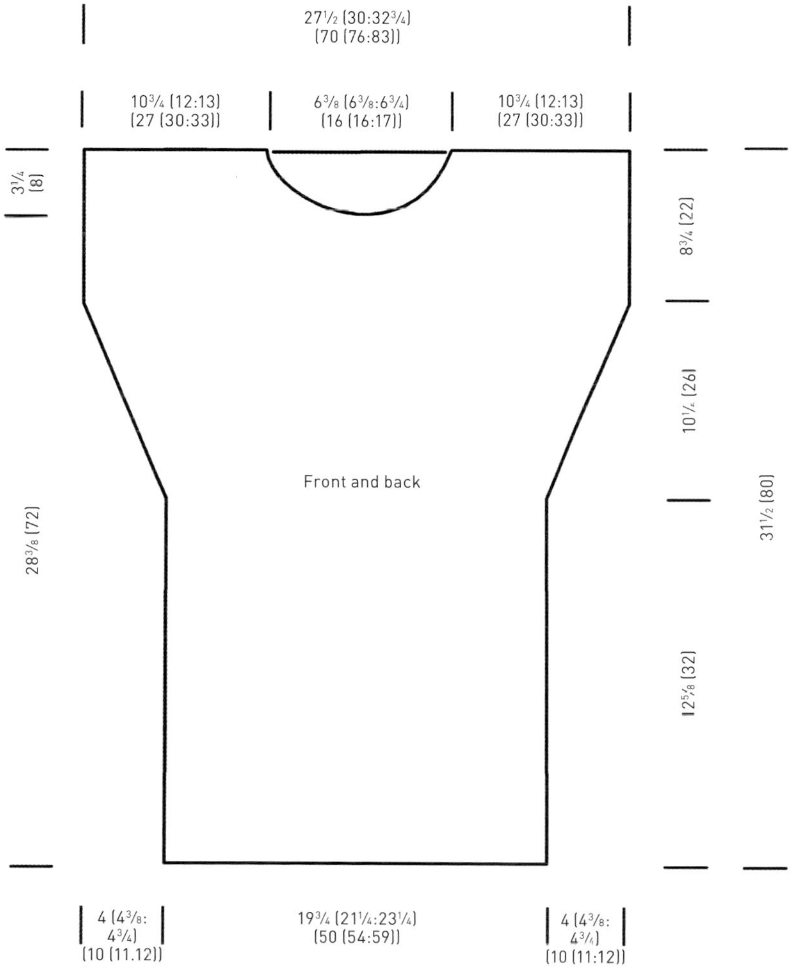

27½ (30:32¾)
(70 (76:83))
10¾ (12:13)
(27 (30:33))
6⅜ (6⅜:6¾)
(16 (16:17))
10¾ (12:13)
(27 (30:33))
3¼
(8)
8¾ (22)
10¼ (26)
Front and back
31½ (80)
28⅜ (72)
12⅝ (32)
4 (4⅜:
4¾)
(10 (11.12))
19¾ (21¼:23¼)
(50 (54:59))
4 (4⅜:
4¾)
(10 (11:12))

Sleeve borders | With the set of 10½in (7mm) double-pointed needles, pick up 54 stitches around the armhole edge and work 1⅝in (4cm) garter stitch in rounds. Cast off all stitches loosely.

Pocket borders | With the set of 10½in (7mm) double-pointed needles, pick up 20 stitches along the side edges and work 1⅝in (4cm) garter stitch in rows. Cast off all stitches loosely.
Sew the side edges to the front at the top and bottom of the pocket.

Finishing | Darn in all the ends.

FOR THE COWL
The cowl is knitted in rounds.
With 10½in (7mm) circular needle, cast on 168 stitches, join into a round, and work knit 12 purl 12 alternately.
When the work measures 14in (35cm), cast off all stitches loosely. Darn in all the ends.

FOR THE WRIST WARMERS
On a set of US10 (6mm) double-pointed needles, cast on 26 stitches, distribute evenly and join into a round. Knit 1 round.
Then work in pattern:
Round 1: *knit 2 together, yarn over needle; repeat from * to end of round.
Rounds 2–4: work in stockinette stitch.
Keep repeating rounds 1–4.
When work measures 9⅝in (24cm), cast off all stitches loosely and darn in all the ends.
Make a second wrist warmer in the same way.

FOR THE HAT
The border is worked first, then the main part of the hat from the border up.

Border | On a set of US10 (6mm) double-pointed needles, cast on 60 stitches, distribute evenly, and join into a round.
Work in knit 1 purl 1 rib. Knit very tightly. After 1⅝in (4cm), cast off all stitches tightly.

Top of hat | With set of US10 (6mm) needles, pick up 90 stitches along the cast-off edge of the band, picking up 1 stitch in the first stitch then 2 stitches in the next stitch, all the way around.
In round 1, work knit 9 purl 9 alternately, ending with purl 9.
Mark the beginning of the round.
Next round: change to US13 (9mm) double-pointed needles. Work 4¾in (12cm) in the broad rib pattern, then start the decreases.

Decrease for top of head | 1st decrease round: knit or purl together the first 2 stitches of all 10 "ribs" (80 stitches remain).
Work 1 round without decreasing.
2nd decrease round: knit or purl together the last 2 stitches of all 10 ribs (70 stitches remain).
Work 1 round without decreasing.
Repeat the 1st and 2nd decreases together with the intervening non-increase round 3 more times, until 10 stitches remain on the needles.
Work a final round without decreasing, then cut the yarn, thread the end through all the stitches and draw together tightly. Darn in all the ends.

Pom-pom | Make a pom-pom (see page 137) about 3¼in (8cm) in diameter and sew it to the top of the hat.

Shades of fall

LONG COAT WITH CABLE PATTERN

GAUGE

10 stitches and 15 rows in stockinette stitch on US15 (10mm/UK000) needles with yarn doubled = 4in (10cm) square.

STITCHES

Stockinette stitch | In rows: right-side rows knit all stitches, wrong-side rows purl all stitches. In rounds: knit all stitches.

Staggered rib | See also chart on page 65. In rows: Right-side rows knit 1, purl 1, wrong-side rows purl 1, knit 1. Work 4 rows, then change to right-side rows purl 1, knit 1 and wrong-side rows knit 1 purl 1. Continue in this way, changing every 4 rows.

Diamond cable | Work from the chart over the 14 stitches between the arrows. The figures to the right refer to the right-side rows. On wrong-side rows, work the stitches as they appear. Starting from the bottom, work rows 1–26 once, then keep repeating rows 5–26.

Rib borders | Knit 2 purl 2 alternately.

LONG COAT WITH CABLE PATTERN
Sizes S, M, L

Measurements for size S are in front of parentheses: sizes M and L are inside parentheses (M:L). If only one measurement is given, it applies to all sizes.

Style: semi-fitted; narrow, but not constricting

MATERIALS

- 16 (18:20) balls of Lana Grossa Alta Moda Alpaca (153yd/50g; 90% alpaca, 5% pure new wool, 5% polyamide) in gray-brown (col. 10)
- US15 (10mm/UK000) circular needles, 24 and 32in (60 and 80cm) long
- Set of US15 (10mm/UK000) double-pointed needles
- Stitch markers or safety pins
- Stitch holder or cable needle
- 1 button, 1¼in (30mm) diameter

TO MAKE

The coat is knitted with double yarn.

Back and front | The coat is knitted in one piece in long rows up to the armholes. With US15 (10mm) circular needle and double yarn, cast on 85 (97:109) stitches.
Allocate the stitches as follows:
1 edge stitch, 19 (22:25) stitches for the front, 45 (51:57) stitches for the back, 19 (22:25) stitches for the left front, 1 edge stitch.
Mark the imaginary side seams with stitch markers or safety pins.
The pattern layout begins at the front edge of the right front: 1 edge stitch, 3 (4:5) stitches staggered rib, 14 stitches diamond cable pattern, 2 (4:6) stitches staggered rib, side seam marker, 5 (7:9) stitches staggered rib, 14 stitches diamond cable pattern, 7 (9:11) stitches staggered rib, 14 stitches diamond cable pattern, 5 (7:9) stitches staggered rib, side seam marker, 2 (4:6) stitches staggered rib, 14 stitches diamond cable pattern, 3 (4:5) stitches staggered rib, 1 edge stitch.

Note | The 3¼in (8cm) wide rib border is knitted on later. The fronts are therefore narrower than the back by half the width of the border, i.e., 1⅝in (4cm), so that the buttonhole and button will be at the center front.

Decrease for the waist | The coat is slightly waisted. Decreases for this are worked at both side seams.
When work measures 19¾ (19:18⅛)in (50 (48:46)cm), knit together the third-to-last and second-to-last stitches of the right front, (i.e., for size S the 17th and 18th stitches, for size M the 20th and 21st stitches and for size L the 23rd and 24th stitches), the second and third stitches of the back, the third-to-last and second-to-last

stitches of the back and the second and third stitches of the left front.
4 stitches are thus decreased in each row.
Repeat the decreases twice more on every 6th row (73 (85:97) stitches remain). Work 7 rows and the increase again by knitting into the front and back of the 2nd stitch before and after the side seams. Repeat the increases twice more on every 8th row, (85 (97:109) stitches on the needle).

Front neck | When work measures 26¾in (68cm), begin decreasing at the neck edge on both fronts. On the right front, slip the third stitch, knit the fourth and pass the slipped stitch over, and on the left front, knit the third-to-last and fourth-to-last stitches together.
Decrease a total of 6 times on every 6th row. Remember to work the armholes as well, when the work measures 31½ (30⅝:30)in (80 (78:76)cm).

Divide for fronts and back | When work measures 31½ (30⅝:30)in (80 (78:76)cm), divide for the armholes and finish the fronts and back separately. Continue casting off at the front neck edges as described above.
The center 45 (51:57) stitches form the back; the remaining stitches make up the right and left fronts. The number of stitches for the fronts may vary, depending on how many stitches have already been cast off at the neck edge.

Back armholes | Finish the back first. At the start of the following 6 rows, work 2 rows each as follows: cast off 2 stitches twice and 1 stitch once (35 (41:47) stitches remain). Continue in pattern.

Charts and pattern

LONG COAT WITH CABLE PATTERN

PATTERN DIAGRAM
Measurements in inches (cm)

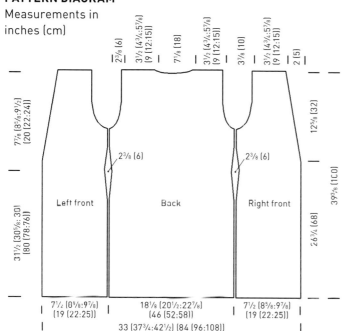

2³⁄₈ (6)

3¹⁄₂ (4³⁄₄:5⁷⁄₈)
(9 (12:15))

7¹⁄₈ (18)

3¹⁄₂ (4³⁄₄:5⁷⁄₈)
(9 (12:15))

3⁷⁄₈ (10)

3¹⁄₂ (4³⁄₄:5⁷⁄₈)
(9 (12:15))

2 (5)

7⁷⁄₈ (8⁵⁄₈:9¹⁄₂)
(20 (22:24))

2³⁄₈ (6)

2³⁄₈ (6)

12⁵⁄₈ (32)

39³⁄₈ (100)

Left front

Back

Right front

31¹⁄₂ (30⁵⁄₈:30)
(80 (78:76))

26³⁄₄ (68)

7¹⁄₂ (8⁵⁄₈:9⁷⁄₈)
(19 (22:25))

18¹⁄₈ (20¹⁄₂:22⁷⁄₈)
(46 (52:58))

7¹⁄₂ (8⁵⁄₈:9⁷⁄₈)
(19 (22:25))

33 (37³⁄₄:42¹⁄₂) (84 (96:108))

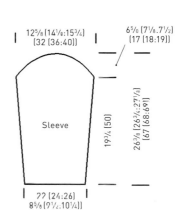

12⁵⁄₈ (14¹⁄₈:15³⁄₄)
(32 (36:40))

6⁵⁄₈ (7¹⁄₈:7¹⁄₂)
(17 (18:19))

Sleeve

19³⁄₄ (50)

26³⁄₈ (26³⁄₄:27¹⁄₃)
(67 (68:69))

22 (24:26)
8⁵⁄₈ (9¹⁄₂:10¹⁄₄)

CHART
Diamond cable pattern

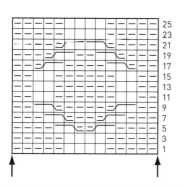

25
23
21
19
17
15
13
11
9
7
5
3
1

CHART
Staggered rib pattern

7
5
3
1

Key:

☐ = Knit 1

⊟ = Purl 1

= Cross 3 right: Slip 1 stitch onto a cable needle and leave at back of work, knit 2, then purl the stitch from the cable needle

= Cross 3 left: Slip 2 stitches onto a cable needle and leave at front of work, purl 1, then knit the 2 stitches from the cable needle

Back neck | When work measures 38½in (98cm), cast off the center 11 stitches. Cast off 3 stitches at each side of the neck on the next row. Slip the remaining 9 (12:15) stitches onto holders for the shoulders. They will later be knitted together with the shoulder stitches of the fronts.

Front armholes | Finish each front separately. Work the armholes as for the back. Continue decreasing at the neck edge. When work measures 39¾in (100cm), slip the remaining 9 (12:15) stitches onto holders for the shoulders. They will later be knitted together with the shoulder stitches of the back.

Join the shoulder seams | Turn the coat to the wrong side and join one shoulder seam by knitting together 1 stitch of the back and 1 stitch of the front shoulder. In the next (wrong-side) row, cast off all stitches. Join the second shoulder seam in the same way. Alternatively, the shoulder stitches can be grafted together or cast off and sewn up later.

Front and neck border | Pick up a total of 270 stitches along the front edges and the back of the neck, starting and ending with purl 2 at the hems. Work in knit 2, purl 2 rib. When 1⅝in (4cm) have been worked, make 1 buttonhole in the right front, 26¾in (68cm) up from the hem, by casting off 2 stitches. In the following wrong-side row, cast on 2 stitches to replace them and work a further 1⅝in (4cm). When the border is 3¼in (8cm) wide, cast off all stitches.

Sleeves | The sleeves are worked in rounds on double-pointed needles, and have no seams. On the set of US15 (10mm) double-pointed needles, cast on 20 (24:28) stitches and distribute evenly. Mark the imaginary seam.

Work 2⅜in (6cm) in knit 2 purl 2 rib. Change to working a diamond cable over the center 14 stitches and the 3 (5:7) stitches on either side in staggered rib. Increase a total of 10 (12:14) stitches for the sleeves, by working 1 stitch into the strand between the second and third stitches and between the third-to-last and second-to-last stitches of the round (i.e., 2 stitches per round). Begin the increases in the 2nd round after the border. Increase a total of 5 (6:7) times in every 7th round working the increases in staggered rib (30 (36:42) stitches on the needles).

Sleeve top | When sleeve measures 19¾in (50cm), change to working in rows. To begin with, it is best to work on two or three needles from the set of double-pointed needles. Later, when fewer stitches remain, one needle will be enough. At the beginning of the following 6 rows, work 2 rows each of the following: cast off 2 stitches twice and 1 stitch once (20 (26:32) stitches remain). Continue without shaping until sleeve measures 24 (24¼:25¼)in (61 (63:64)cm). Then at the start of the next 8 rows, work 2 rows each of the following: cast off 1-1-2-4 stitches for size S, 1-2-3-4 stitches for size M and 2-2-3-5 stitches for size L. Cast off the remaining 4 (6:8) stitches on the next right-side row.

Finishing | Sew in the sleeves. Darn in all the ends. Sew on the button.

Winter warmers

PONCHO WITH HAT AND LEG WARMERS

GAUGE
10 stitches and 15 rows in stockinette stitch on
US15 (10mm/UK000) needles = 4in (10cm) square.

STITCHES
Stockinette stitch | In rounds: knit all stitches.
Rib borders | Knit 2 purl 2 alternately.
Diamond cable | Work from the chart on page 71
over the 14 stitches between the arrows. The
figures to the right refer to the pattern rows.
On wrong-side rows, work the stitches as they
appear. Starting from the bottom, keep repeating
rows 1–28.
Cable pattern | Working from the chart on page
71, begin with the 6 stitches between the arrows.
The figures to the right refer to the pattern
rounds. On the rounds in between, work the
stitches as stockinette stitch. Starting from the
bottom, work rounds 1 to 16 once, then repeat
rounds 9–16 four times (48 rounds in total). Then
work rounds 49–78 once.

FOR THE PONCHO
The poncho is knitted in one piece in rounds from
the bottom up, with a cable running down each arm.

Rib border | With the 40in- (100cm-) long US15
(10mm) circular needle cast on 164 stitches and
work 4in (10cm) in knit 2 purl 2 rib.

PONCHO WITH HAT AND LEG WARMERS
One size
Style: generous
Hat: to fit head size 21–22½in
(53–57cm)

MATERIALS
- 10 balls Lana Grossa Alta Moda Super
  Baby (66yd/50g; 67% wool, 30%
  Alpaca, 3% nylon) in dark red (col. 20)
  for poncho, 2 balls for hat, and 3 balls
  for leg warmers
- US15 (10mm/UK000) circular
  needles, 24, 32, and 40in (60, 80, and
  100cm) long
- US13 (9mm/UK00) and US15 (10mm/
  UK000) double-pointed needles
- Safety pin or spare yarn
- 1 cable needle
- 1 fur pom-pom

Stitch layout for the cables | After the border, allocate the stitches as follows: 68 stitches stockinette stitch for the back, 14 stitches for the left arm with diamond cable pattern from the chart, 68 stitches stockinette stitch for the front, and 14 stitches for the right arm with diamond cable pattern from the chart. Mark the beginning of the rounds where the back meets the right arm. Work one round as described.

Decreases | Decrease by knitting together the second and third stitches and the third-to-last and second-to-last stitches of the stockinette stitch back and front (i.e., 4 stitches in each decrease round). Work the decreases at the start of the back and front as slip 1, knit 1, pass slipped stitch over (see page 134) and those at the end as knit 2 together. Decrease in 2 successive rounds, then work 1 round without decreasing and repeat. This means that the number of stitches is reduced by 8 for every 3 rounds. Continue decreasing in this way until 52 stitches remain.

Roll collar | After an 18th round of the chart, when the work measures about 19¾in (50cm) and 52 stitches remain, change to knit 2 purl 2 rib

> **Tip**
>
> The poncho can also be worn with the diamond cable pattern at the front and back, as shown in the photo on page 68.

for the roll collar. When the collar measures 9½in (24cm), cast off all stitches loosely.

Finishing | Darn in all the ends.

FOR THE HAT
On the set of US13 (9mm) double-pointed needles, cast on 52 stitches and distribute evenly. Work 12⅝in (32cm) in knit 2 purl 2 rib (26 ribs). Decrease for the top as follows:
1st decrease round: purl together the two stitches of all the purl ribs (39 stitches remain). Work 1 round without decreasing.
2nd decrease round: knit together the two stitches of all the knit ribs (26 stitches remain). Work 1 round without decreasing.
3rd decrease round: knit 2 together, purl 2 together to end of round (13 stitches remain). Knit 1 round.
Cut the yarn, leaving a long end, thread it through all the stitches, draw the top of the hat together and fasten off on the inside. Attach the pom-pom.

FOR THE LEG WARMERS
The leg warmers are knitted from the knee down.
On the set of US15 (10mm) double-pointed needles, cast on 40 stitches and allocate the stitches as follows: 6 stitches from the chart, *purl 2, knit 2*, repeat from * to * twice more, purl 2, 6 stitches from the chart, *purl 2, knit 2 *, repeat from * to * twice more, purl 2. Work rounds 1–16 of the chart with these repetitions 3 times in all.
On round 53, reduce each of the cables to 4 stitches by knitting 2 stitches together twice, and continue working from the chart.
When work measures 13½in (34cm), cast off all stitches loosely. Darn in all the ends.
Make the second leg warmer in the same way.

Charts and pattern

CHART
Diamond cable pattern

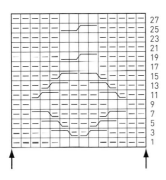

27
25
23
21
19
17
15
13
11
9
7
5
3
1

Key:

 – Knit 1

– Purl 1

= Knit 2 together

= Cross 3 right: Slip 1 stitch onto a cable needle and leave at back of work, knit 2, then purl the stitch from the cable needle

= Cross 3 left: Slip 2 stitches onto a cable needle and leave at front of work, purl 1, then knit the 2 stitches from the cable needle

= Cable 4 back: Slip 2 stitches onto a cable needle and leave at back of work, knit 2, then knit the 2 stitches from the cable needle

= Cable 6 back: Slip 3 stitches onto a cable needle and leave at back of work, knit 3, then knit the 3 stitches from the cable needle

CHART
Cable pattern for leg warmers

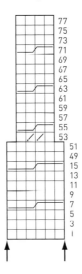

77
75
73
71
69
67
65
63
61
59
57
55
53

51
49
15
13
11
9
7
5
3
1

PATTERN DIAGRAM
Measurements in inches (cm)

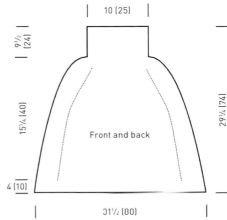

10 (25)

9½ (24)

15¼ (40)

29¼ (74)

Front and back

4 (10)

31½ (80)

Subtle neutrals

*SWEATER WITH HAT
AND CHILD'S SHOULDER WARMER*

GAUGE

8 stitches and 16 rows in garter stitch on
US17 (12mm) needles = 4in (10cm) square.

STITCHES

Garter stitch | In rows: knit all stitches.
In rounds: 1 round knit and 1 round purl
alternately.
Rib border | knit 1 purl 1 alternately.
Hat border | knit 2 purl 2 alternately.

FOR THE SWEATER

Back and front | The sweater is worked in one
piece in rounds up to the armholes. On the US15
(10mm) circular needle, cast on 80 (90:100)
stitches, join into a round and work 2in (5cm) in
knit 1 purl 1 rib. Mark the imaginary seams with
stitch markers or safety pins. The front and back
each consist of 40 (45:50) stitches. The rounds
begin at the right edge of the front.
When ribbing measures 2in (5cm), change to the
US17 (12mm) needle and garter stitch.

Divide for front and back | When work measures
17³⁄₄ (17³⁄₈:17)in (45 (44:43)cm), divide for the
armholes and finish the back and front
separately, working in rows. Divide the front and
back into 40 (45:50) stitches for each and finish
the back first.

SWEATER WITH HAT AND CHILD'S SHOULDER WARMER
Sizes S, M, L
Measurements are S (M:L) If one
measurement is given, it applies to all.
Style: relaxed to oversized
Hat: to fit head size 21¼–22³⁄₄in
(53–57cm)
Shoulder warmer: size 46³⁄₈–51¼in
(116–128cm)

MATERIALS

- 16 (17:18) balls of Lana Grossa
  Ragazza Lei (44yd/50g; 100%
  merino) in cream (col. 14) for
  sweater, 3 balls for hat, and 4 balls
  for shoulder warmer
- US15 (10mm/UK000) and US17
  (12mm) circular needles, 32in
  (80cm) long
- Sets of US13 (9mm/UK00), US15
  (10mm/UK000) and US17 (12mm)
  double-pointed needles
- Stitch markers or safety pins
- Stitch holders or spare needles

Pattern

PATTERN DIAGRAM FOR SWEATER
Measurements in inches (cm)

PATTERN DIAGRAM FOR SHOULDER WARMER
Measurements in inches (cm)

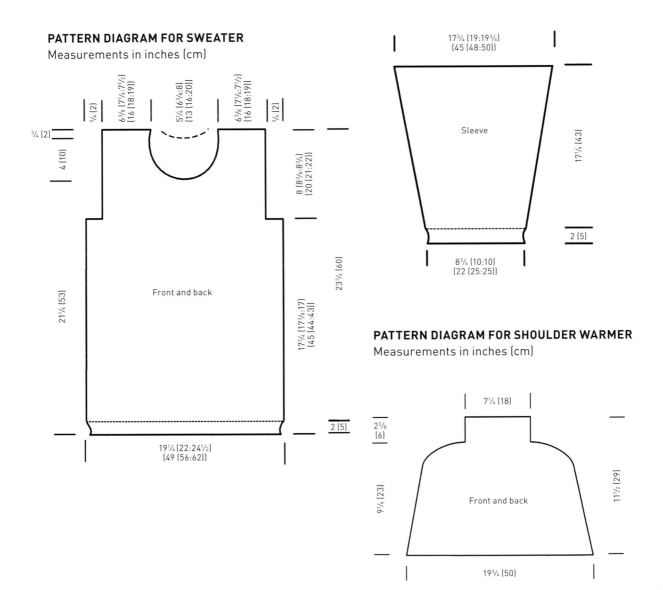

Armholes | Back and front alike: cast off 2 stitches at the beginning of the next two rows (36 (41:46) stitches remain). Continue without further shaping.

Back neck | When work measures 24¾in (63cm), cast off the center 6 (9:12) stitches and finish each side separately by casting off 2 stitches at the neck edge on the following right-side rows. Slip the remaining 13 (14:15) stitches onto holders for the shoulders. They will later be knitted together with the shoulder stitches of the fronts.

Front neck | When work measures 21in (53cm), cast off the center 6 (9:12) stitches. Finish the right and left sides separately by casting off 1 stitch twice at the neck edge on every other row. Continue without shaping until work measures 25½in (65cm) and slip the 13 (14:15) shoulder stitches onto holders as for the back.

Join the shoulder seams | Turn the sweater to the wrong side and join one shoulder seam by knitting together 1 stitch of the back and 1 stitch of the front shoulder. In the next (wrong-side) row, cast off all stitches.
Join the second shoulder seam in the same way. Alternatively, the shoulder stitches can be grafted together or cast off and sewn up later.

Neck border | On the set of US15 (10mm) double-pointed needles, pick up 6 (9:12) stitches of the back neck, 23 (20:17) stitches down the side of the front, 6 (9:12) stitches cast off for the front neck and 23 (20:17) stitches up the other side of the front. (58 stitches). Work 1¼in (3cm) in knit 1 purl 1 rib, then cast off all stitches loosely.

Sleeves | The sleeves are knitted in rounds, with no seam, on a set of double-pointed needles. With US15 (10mm) needles, cast on 18 (20:20) stitches, distribute evenly, and work 2in (5cm) in knit 1 purl 1 rib. Mark the imaginary seam. Change to the set of US17 (12mm) double-pointed needles and garter stitch. Increase in the 3rd round of garter stitch, and every following 7th round, by knitting into the strand between the second and third stitches and the third-to-last and second-to-last stitches of the round. Work a total of 9 (9:10) increases (36 (38:40) stitches). When work measures 19in (48cm), cast off all stitches loosely.

Finishing | Sew in the sleeves. Darn in all the ends.

FOR THE HAT

The hat is knitted from the border up.

With a set of US 13 (9mm) double-pointed needles, cast on 40 stitches and distribute evenly.

Work 2⅜in (6cm) in knit 2 purl 2 rib. In the last round of the border, increase 5 stitches, evenly spaced (45 stitches). Change to the set of US17 (12mm) double-pointed needles and work in garter stitch, beginning with 1 round purl. Work 5¼in (13cm) in garter stitch.

When work measures 7½in (19cm) (border plus 5¼in (13cm)), begin decreasing for the top, until the last remaining stitches can be drawn together.

Note that the decreases are always worked on a purl round.

1st decrease round: purl every 4th and 5th stitch together, then knit 1 round without shaping (36 stitches remain).

2nd decrease round: purl every 3rd and 4th stitch together, then knit 1 round without shaping (27 stitches remain).

3rd decrease round: purl every 2nd and 3rd stitch together, then knit 1 round without shaping (18 stitches remain).

4th decrease round: purl 2 together to end of round (9 stitches remain).

Cut the yarn, leaving an end about 20in (50cm) long and thread this through the remaining stitches. Draw tight, bring the yarn end through to the wrong side and darn in firmly.

Darn in all other ends.

FOR THE SHOULDER WARMER

With the set of US17 (12mm) double-pointed needles, cast on 28 stitches, distribute evenly and work 2⅜in (6cm) in rounds in knit 1 purl 1 rib. In the last round of ribbing, increase 4 stitches evenly spaced (32 stitches).

Change to garter stitch.

Divide the stitches, marking the divisions with stitch markers: 10 stitches for the back, 6 stitches for the right sleeve, 10 stitches for the front and 6 stitches for the left sleeve.

The rounds begin at the join between the left sleeve and the back.

Increase in the front and back on every 3rd round 12 times, working make 1 stitch by knitting into the strand between the two stitches before the marker for the start of each sleeve, and after the marker for the end of each sleeve (i.e., 4 stitches on each increase round). The front and back will get wider, while the sleeves remain the same. When 9¼in (23cm) in garter stitch has been worked, there should be 80 stitches on the needles.

Cast off all stitches loosely and darn in the ends.

Woodland walk

CASUAL RIBBED JACKET

GAUGE

11 stitches and 16 rows in knit 2 purl 2 rib on
US11 (8mm/UK0) needles = 4in (10cm) square.

STITCH

Double rib | In rounds: knit 2 purl 2 alternately.
In rows: knit 2 purl 2 alternately. On wrong-side
rows, work the stitches as they appear.

TO MAKE

Back and front | The jacket is knitted in one piece
in long rows up to the armholes. With the US11
(8mm) circular needle, cast on 154 (170:186)
stitches and work in knit 2 purl 2 rib. Start with a
wrong-side row, beginning and ending with purl 2.

Stitch allocation for front and back |
22 stitches for the right border, 27 (31:35)
stitches for the right front, 56 (64:72) stitches for
the back, 27 (31:35) stitches for the left front, 22
stitches for the left border.
Mark the imaginary side seams in the center of a
knit rib, so that the fronts and back begin and end
with knit 1 on either side of the marker.
Work 22in (56cm) in rib without shaping.

CASUAL RIBBED JACKET
Sizes S, M, L
Measurements for size S are in
front of parentheses: sizes M and L
are inside parentheses (M:L). If only
one measurement is given, it applies
to all sizes.
Style: casual and cozy

MATERIALS

- 7 (8:9) balls of Lana Grossa Yak
  Merino (120yd/50g; 28% alpaca,
  30% pure new wool, 20% yak,
  22% nylon) in petrol (col. 3)
- US11 (8mm/UK0) circular needle,
  32in (80cm) long
- Set of US11 (8mm/UK0) double-
  pointed needles
- Stitch holders or spare needles
- Stitch markers or safety pins

Pattern

PATTERN DIAGRAM
Measurements in inches (cm)

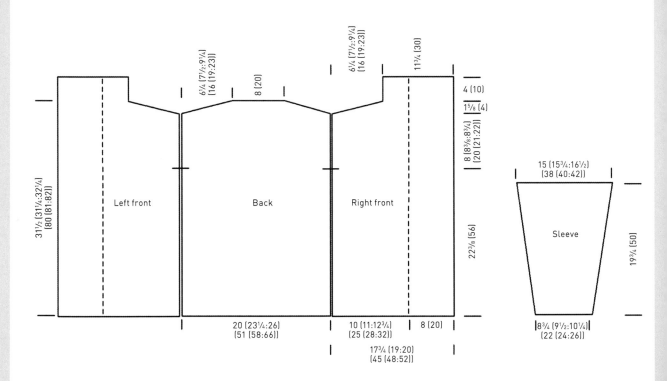

Divide for back and fronts | When work measures 22in (56cm), divide for the armholes, finishing the back and fronts separately.

Back | For the back, continue in rib on the center 56 (64:72) stitches.
When work measures 30 (30³⁄₈:30³⁄₄)in (76 (77:78)cm), cast off the center 22 stitches, leaving 17 (21:25) stitches for each shoulder. Finish the shoulders separately as follows: at the armhole edge on every other row, slip first 5 (7:8) stitches, then 5 (7:8) stitches, and lastly 7 (7:9) stitches onto safety pins. They will later be knitted together with the shoulder stitches of the fronts.

Fronts | Finish the fronts separately. Continue in rib on 49 (53:57) stitches. When the work measures 30 (30³⁄₈:31³⁄₄)in (76 (77:78)cm), slip the 17 (21:25) shoulder stitches at the armhole edge onto holders, as for the back. They will later be knitted together with the shoulder stitches of the fronts.

Join the shoulder seams | Turn the jacket to the wrong side and join one shoulder seam by knitting together 1 stitch of the back and 1 stitch of the front shoulder.
In the next (wrong-side) row, cast off all stitches. Join the second shoulder seam in the same way. Alternatively, the shoulder stitches can be grafted together or cast off and sewn up later.

Finish the borders | On both fronts, work 4in (10cm) in rib on the remaining 32 stitches without shaping. Cast off all stitches and sew the ends together. Sew the border to the back of the neck.

Sleeves | The sleeves are worked in rounds, with no seam, on the set of double-pointed needles.
On the set of 8mm double-pointed needles, cast on 24 (26:28) stitches, distribute evenly and close into a round.
Note: The rib pattern will only divide exactly for sizes S and L at the start. Because of the increases, the rib pattern next to the "seam" will change several times.
Mark the imaginary seam with a stitch marker or safety pin.
Increase in every 7th round 9 times, by knitting into the strand between the second and third stitches and the third-to-last and second-to-last stitches of the round (42 (44:46) stitches).
When sleeve measures 19³⁄₄in (50cm), cast off all stitches.

Finishing | Sew in the sleeves. Darn in all the ends.

Nature lover

MINI VEST IN MOSS STITCH

GAUGE
10 stitches and 15 rows in moss stitch on US15 (10mm/UK000) needles = 4in (10cm) square.

STITCH
Moss stitch | Knit 1 purl 1 alternately. On the next row, move along by 1 stitch, so purl the knit stitches and knit the purl stitches.

TO MAKE
Back | On a US15 (10mm) circular needle, cast on 43 (45:47) stitches and work in moss stitch.

Increase for wide sleeves | When work measures 7¼in (18cm), at the end of the next 6 rows, 2 rows each of the following: cast on 2–3–5 stitches, working the stitches into the moss stitch pattern (63 (65:67) stitches). Continue in moss stitch until work measures 15⅜in (39cm).

Back neck | Next row: work 24 (25:26) stitches, cast off 15 stitches and work 24 (25:26) stitches.

Fronts | Slip the 24 (25:26) stitches for the right front onto a holder and finish the left front first. Work 6¾in (17cm) from the back neck in moss stitch. Then in every other row, at the side-seam edge, cast off 5–3–2 stitches, corresponding to the sleeve increases for the back (14 (15:16) stitches remain).

When work measures 15⅜in (39cm) from the back neck, cast off all remaining stitches loosely. Work the right front to match.

Finishing | Place the back and fronts right sides together, and sew up the side seams. Darn in all the ends.

MINI VEST IN MOSS STITCH
Sizes S, M, L
Measurements for size S are in front of parentheses: sizes M and L are inside parentheses (M:L). If only one measurement is given, it applies to all sizes.
Style: casual

MATERIALS
- 3 (4:4) balls of Lion Brand Wool-Ease Thick and Quick (106yd/170g; 80% acrylic, 20% wool) in Denim
- US15 (10mm/UK000) circular needle, 32in (80cm) long
- Stitch holder or spare needle

Pattern

MINI VEST

PATTERN DIAGRAM
Measurements in inches (cm)

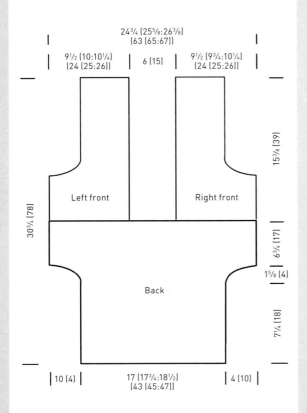

24¾ (25⅝:26⅜)
(63 (65:67))

9½ (10:10¼)
(24 (25:26))

6 (15)

9½ (9¾:10¼)
(24 (25:26))

15⅜ (39)

Left front

Right front

30¾ (78)

6¾ (17)

1⅝ (4)

Back

7¼ (18)

10 (4)

17 (17¾:18½)
(43 (45:47))

4 (10)

Pattern

BODY WARMER

PATTERN DIAGRAM
Measurements in inches (cm)

Before folding

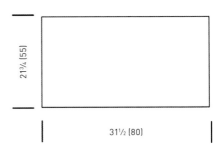

21¾ (55)

31½ (80)

After folding

5½ (14) 6 (15) 8¾ (22) 6 (15) 5½ (14)

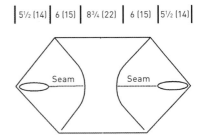

Seam

Seam

Riverside ramble

SIMPLE BODY WARMER

GAUGE
7 stitches and 9 rows in stockinette stitch on US17 (12mm) needles with yarn tripled = 4in (10cm) square.

STITCHES
Stockinette stitch | Right-side rows knit all stitches, wrong-side rows purl all stitches.
Edge stitches | Slip the 1st stitch of every row knitwise and knit the last stitch.

TO MAKE
The yarn is used triple: two strands camel/black and one strand lilac/black.
With US17 (12mm) circular needle, cast on 56 stitches and work in stockinette stitch, beginning with a wrong-side row (purl all stitches).
When work measures 21⅝in (55cm), cast off all stitches loosely on a right-side row.

Armholes | Place the piece wrong-side up. Put top-right and bottom-right edges together and sew 6in (15cm) of the cast-on and cast-off edges together. Do the same with the two left edges. This produces a piece with armholes 5½in (14cm) long and 11in (28cm) in circumference.

Finishing | Darn in all the ends.

SIMPLE BODY WARMER
One size
Style: casual
The size of the body warmer is easy to change. The width of the piece of knitting gives the width from armhole to armhole. If you would prefer the sleeves to reach to the middle of the forearm, cast on about 20 more stitches. The height of the piece of knitting gives the back length.
For pattern diagram, see page 84.

MATERIALS
- 1 ball of Lana Grossa Garzato Fleece (246yd/50g; 70% alpaca, 30% nylon) in lilac/black (col. 007) and 2 balls in camel/black (col. 006)
- US17 (12mm) circular needle, 32in (80cm) long

Home comforts

IT'S THE WEEKEND AT LAST! ALL YOU NEED TO HELP YOU KICK BACK AND RELAX IS A GOOD BOOK, A CUP OF FRAGRANT HERBAL TEA…AND A COZY SWEATER TO SNUGGLE IN.

Lazy days

STOCKINETTE-STITCH SWEATER WITH SCARF

GAUGE

9 stitches and 15 rows in stockinette stitch on
US11 (8mm/UK0) needles = 4in (10cm) square.

STITCHES

Stockinette stitch | In rows: right-side rows knit
all stitches, wrong-side rows purl all stitches.
In rounds: knit all stitches.
Rib borders | Knit 2 purl 2 alternately.

FOR THE SWEATER

Back and front | The sweater is worked in one
piece on the circular needle up to the armholes.
On the US11 (8mm) circular needle, cast on
84 (92:100) stitches and work 3¼in (8cm) in
knit 2 purl 2 rib.
Change to stockinette stitch.

Divide for front and back | When work measures
19¼ (18¾:18⅜)in (48 (47:46)cm), divide for the
front and back, 42 (46:50) stitches for each.
Continue in rows.

Armholes | Finish the back first. Cast off
4 stitches at the beginning of the next two rows
(34 (38:42) stitches remain). Continue without
shaping until work measures 26⅜in (66cm), then
cast off all stitches.

STOCKINETTE-STITCH SWEATER WITH SCARF

Sizes S, M, L

Measurements for size S are in front
of parentheses: sizes M and L are
inside parentheses (M:L). If only one
measurement is given, it applies to
all sizes.
Style: semi-fitted
Scarf: 10¼in (26cm) wide, 80in
(200cm) long

MATERIALS

- 8 (9:10) balls of Lana Grossa
  Bombolo (71yd/50g; 30% mohair,
  20% pure new wool, 40% acrylic,
  10% nylon) in beige (col. 1) for
  sweater and 4 balls for scarf
- US11 (8mm/UK0) circular needle,
  32in (80cm) long
- Set of US11 (8mm/UK0)
  double-pointed needles
- Stitch holders or spare needles

Pattern

STOCKINETTE-STITCH SWEATER

PATTERN DIAGRAM
Measurements
in inches (cm)

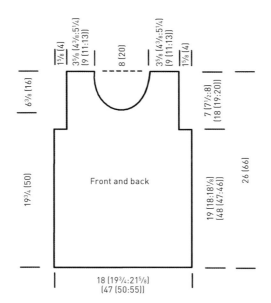

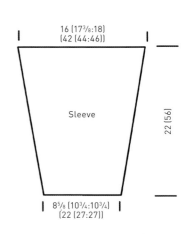

Front neck | Now finish the front. Cast off for the armholes as for the back (see page 91). When the work measures 19¾in (50cm), cast off the center 10 stitches, leaving 12 (14:16) stitches on each side. Finish the right and left fronts separately. Cast off at the neck edge on every other row 2 stitches once and 1 stitch twice, or slip the stitches onto safety pins.
When work measures 26in (66cm), cast off 8 (10:12) stitches for the shoulders or slip them onto a holder.

Sleeves | Cast on 20 (24:24) stitches and either transfer to a set of double-pointed needles or knit the sleeve on two needles and sew up the seam later. Work 2⅜in (6cm) in knit 2 purl 2 rib, then change to stockinette stitch.

In every 5th row, increase by making 1 in the strand between the third and fourth stitches and the fourth-to-last and third-to-last stitches of the row. Work a total of 9 (8:9) increases (38 (40:42) stitches on needle). When sleeve measures 22in (56cm), cast off all stitches loosely.

Finishing | Sew up the shoulder and sleeve seams. Sew the sleeves in loosely. Pick up 40 stitches evenly around the neck edge and work 1¼in (3cm) in knit 2 purl 2 rib. Cast off all stitches loosely.

FOR THE SCARF
With the US11 (8mm) circular needle, cast on 24 stitches and work in stockinette stitch in rows. When the scarf measures 80in (200cm), cast off all stitches loosely.

Sheer elegance

PRETTY WRAPAROUND CARDIGAN

GAUGE

8 stitches and 13 rows in stockinette stitch on US17 (12mm) needles = 4in (10cm) square.

STITCHES

Stockinette stitch | In rows: right-side rows knit all stitches, wrong-side rows purl all stitches. In rounds: knit all stitches.

TO MAKE

Back and front | The cardigan is worked in one piece in long rows up to the armholes. On the US17 (12mm) circular needle, cast on 102 (106:110) stitches and work 8in (20cm) in stockinette stitch, starting with a purl (wrong-side) row.

Work the first stitch of every row as an edge stitch. On right-side rows, slip this stitch knitwise and on wrong-side rows, slip the first stitch purlwise.

The stitches are divided as follows: 15 stitches for the right-front wraparound panel, 18 (19:20) stitches for the right front, 36 (38:40) stitches for the back, 18 (19:20) stitches for the left front, and 15 stitches for the left wraparound panel.

Mark the imaginary side seams with stitch markers or safety pins

PRETTY WRAPAROUND CARDIGAN
Sizes S, M, L
Measurements for size S are in front of parentheses: sizes M and L are inside parentheses (M:L). If only one measurement is given, it applies to all sizes.
Style: close-fitting

MATERIALS

- 9 (10:11) balls of Lana Grossa Linea Pura Cashsilk (82yd/50g; 15% silk, 15% cashmere, 30% bamboo, 40% nylon) in sage (col. 37)
- US17 (12mm) circular needle, 32in (80cm) long
- Set of US17 (12mm) double-pointed needles
- US K-10½ (7mm/UK2) crochet hook or French knitter
- Stitch holders or spare needles
- Stitch markers or safety pins

Pattern

PRETTY WRAPAROUND CARDIGAN

PATTERN DIAGRAM
Measurements in inches (cm)

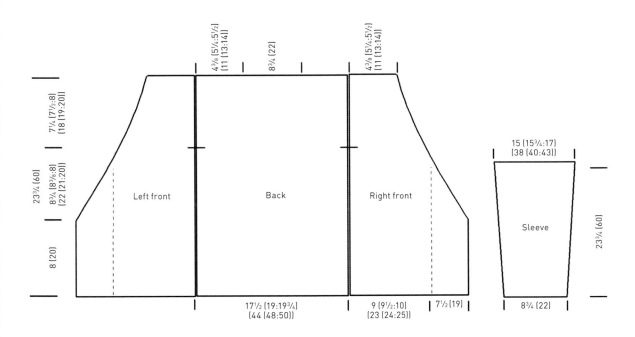

Hole for tie belt | When work measures 8in (20cm), on a right-side row cast off the 33rd and 34th stitches and cast them on again in the following wrong-side row.

Decrease for front edges | Now, at the beginning of every right-side row, work the third and fourth stitches as slip 1, knit 1, pass slipped stitch over and at the end of the row knit the fourth-to-last and third-to-last stitches together.

Divide for fronts and back | When work measures 16½ (16¼:15¾)in (42 (41:40)cm), divide for the armholes and finish the fronts and back separately. The center 36 (38:40) stitches form the back. Divide the remaining stitches by two for the fronts.
The number of stitches for the fronts will vary, depending on how many decreases have been worked.

Back | Finish the back first. Work without shaping until the back measures 23¾in (60cm), then cast off the center 18 stitches and slip 9 (10:11) stitches at each side onto holders for the shoulders.

Fronts | Work as for the back, while continuing to decrease at the front edge until 9 (10:11) stitches remain on the needle. Slip these stitches onto holders.

Join the shoulder seams | Turn the cardigan to the wrong side and join one shoulder seam by knitting together 1 stitch of the back and 1 stitch of the front shoulder and cast off. Join the second shoulder seam in the same way.
Alternatively, the shoulder stitches can be grafted together or cast off and sewn up later.

Tie belt | With the US K-10½ (7mm) crochet hook, make a chain 43¼ (45¼:47½)in (110 (115:120)cm) long and work a row of single crochet into it. Alternatively, you can make a belt with a French knitter or by twisting the yarn into a cord. Make a second belt in the same way and sew the belts to the fronts, 8in (20cm) from the bottom edge.

Sleeves | The sleeves are knitted in rounds with no seam, on the set of double-pointed needles. On the set of US17 (12mm) double-pointed needles, cast on 18 stitches, distribute evenly and mark the imaginary seam with a stitch marker or safety pin.

Sleeve increases | For size S, increase on every 4th round 6 times by making 1 in the strand between the second and third stitches and the third-to-last and second-to-last stitches (30 stitches on needles).
For size M, increase 7 times on every 4th round (32 stitches).
For size L, increase 8 times, in every 3rd and 4th round alternately (34 stitches).
When sleeve measures 23¾in (60cm), cast off all stitches.

Finishing | Sew in the sleeves. Darn in all the ends. Block according to instructions on ball band. Leave the cardigan to dry under a damp cloth.

Soft and silky

*OPEN JACKET WITH MOSS-STITCH BORDERS
AND MATCHING SCARF*

GAUGE
9.5 stitches and 16 rows in stockinette stitch on
US15 (10mm/UK000) needles = 4in (10cm) square.

STITCHES
Stockinette stitch | In rows: right-side rows knit
all stitches, wrong-side rows purl all stitches.
In rounds: knit all stitches.
Moss stitch | Knit 1 purl 1 alternately. On the next
row, move along by 1 stitch, so purl the knit
stitches and knit the purl stitches.

FOR THE JACKET
Back and fronts | The jacket is worked in one
piece in long rows up to the armholes. On US15
(10mm) circular needle, cast on 104 (116:128)
stitches and work a 1⅝in (4cm) border in moss
stitch.
Change to stockinette stitch.
Divide the stitches as follows: 4 stitches for right
front border in moss stitch, 24 (27:30) stitches for
the right front, 48 (54:60) stitches for the back,
24 (27:30) stitches for the left front, and
4 stitches for the left front border in moss
stitch (104 (116:128) stitches).
Mark the imaginary side seams with stitch
markers or safety pins.

OPEN JACKET AND MATCHING SCARF
Sizes S, M, L
Measurements for size S are in front
of parentheses: sizes M and L are
inside parentheses (M:L). If only one
measurement is given, it applies to
all sizes.
Style: casual, comfy
Scarf: 71in (180cm) long,
11¼in (28cm) wide

MATERIALS
- 10 (12:13) balls of Lana Grossa
  Linea Pura Cashsilk (82yd/50g;
  40% nylon, 30%, bamboo, 15%
  cashmere, 15% silk) in lilac (col.
  40) for jacket and 6 balls for scarf
- US15 (10mm/UK000) circular
  needles, 32 and 40in (80 and
  100cm) long
- Set of US15 (10mm/UK000)
  double-pointed needles
- US17 (12mm) circular needle,
  24in (60cm) long for scarf
- Stitch markers or safety pins
- Stitch holders or spare needles

Front slope | When work measures 15in (38cm), begin decreasing at both front neck edges. On the right front, work the second and third stitches after the border (i.e., the 6th and 7th stitches from the beginning of the row) as slip 1 knit 1, pass slipped stitch over (see page 134) and on the left front, knit together the third-to-last and second-to-last stitches before the border. Decrease on every 4th row a total of 9 times, until there are 15 (18:21) shoulder stitches plus 4 border stitches remaining on the needle. Remember to divide for the armholes when the work measures 20 (19⅝:19¼)in (50 (49:48)cm).

Divide for fronts and back | When the work measures 19¾ (19¼:19)in (50 (49:48)cm), divide for the armholes and finish the fronts and back separately. The center 48 (54:60) stitches form the back.

Finish the back | Finish the back first, continuing to work in stockinette stitch without shaping. When the work measures 27½in (70cm), cast off the center 18 stitches and slip the remaining 15 (18:21) stitches at each side onto holders for the shoulders. They will later be knitted together with the shoulder stitches of the fronts.

Finish the fronts | Finish the fronts separately. Work in stockinette stitch and continue decreasing as described above until 15 (18:21) shoulder stitches plus the 4 stitches of the border remain (19 (21:24) stitches). When work measures 28in (70cm), slip the 15 (18:21) knit stitches for the shoulders onto a holder. They will later be knitted together with the shoulder stitches of the back.

Join the shoulder seams | Turn the jacket to the wrong side and join one shoulder seam by knitting together 1 stitch of the back and 1 stitch of the front shoulder and casting off. Join the second shoulder seam in the same way. Alternatively, the shoulder stitches can be grafted together or cast off and sewn up later.

Border | Continue on the 4 stitches of the border for 4in (10cm) on each front, first increasing 1 stitch at the neck edge side, which will later be used as a seam allowance. Knit the ends of the borders together and sew the border to the back neck edge.

Sleeves | The sleeves are knitted in rounds with no seam, on double-pointed needles. On the set of 10mm double-pointed needles, cast on 24 (26:28) stitches and distribute evenly. Mark the imaginary seam with a stitch marker or a safety pin. Work 1⅝in (4cm) in moss stitch.

Tip

With this yarn, always start a new ball at the edge of a row, since the yarn structure means you cannot sew through the knitted stitches. Darned-in ends will be less visible at the edges of the work.

Pattern

PATTERN DIAGRAM
Measurements in inches (cm)

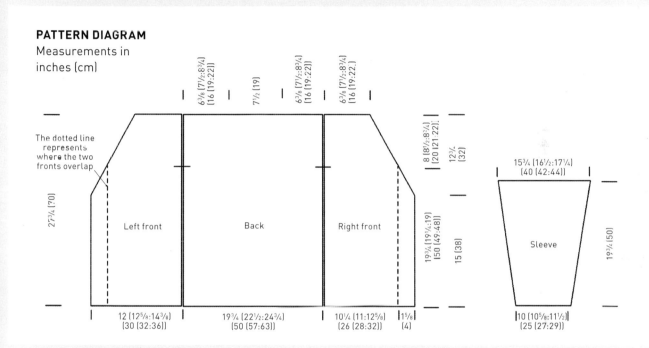

The dotted line represents where the two fronts overlap

6³/₈ (7¹/₂:8³/₄) [16 (19:22)]

7¹/₂ [19]

6³/₈ (7¹/₂:8³/₄) [16 (19:22)]

6³/₈ (7¹/₂:8³/₄) [16 (19:22)]

8 (8¹/₂:8³/₄) [20 (21:22)]

12³/₄ (32)

27³/₄ [70]

19³/₄ (19¹/₄:19) [50 (49:48)]

15 [38]

Left front

Back

Right front

Sleeve

15³/₄ (16¹/₂:17¹/₄) [40 (42:44)]

19³/₄ [50]

12 (12⁵/₈:14³/₈) [30 (32:36)]

19³/₄ (22¹/₂:24³/₄) [50 (57:63)]

10¹/₄ (11:12⁵/₈) [26 (28:32)]

1⁵/₈ (4)

10 (10⁵/₈:11¹/₂) [25 (27:29)]

Sleeve increases | Work the increases by making 1 in the strand between the second and third stitches and between the third-to-last and second-to-last stitches of the round.
Increase at each end of every 7th round a total of 7 times (38 (40:42) stitches on needles).
When sleeve measures 19³/₄in (50cm), cast off all stitches loosely.

Finishing | Sew in the sleeves. Darn in all the ends.

FOR THE SCARF
On the US17 (12mm) circular needle, cast on 29 stitches.
Work in rows in moss stitch, beginning and ending each row with purl 1.
When the scarf measures 71in (180cm), cast off all stitches loosely and darn in the ends.

Relax to the max

LONG HOODED COAT

GAUGE

9 stitches and 16 rows in stockinette stitch on US13 (9mm/UK00) needles = 4in (10cm) square.

STITCHES

Stockinette stitch | In rows: right-side rows knit all stitches, wrong-side rows purl all stitches. In rounds: knit all stitches
Rib border | Knit 1 purl 1 alternately.

TO MAKE

Back and front | The coat is knitted in one piece in rows up to the armholes. On the US13 (9mm) circular needle, cast on 113 (125:137) stitches and work 2³⁄₈in (6cm) in knit 1 purl 1 rib. Start with a wrong-side row, beginning and ending with purl. Change to stockinette stitch, except for the rib borders. In the first row of stockinette stitch, increase 1 stitch by knitting into the front and back of the 40th (43rd:46th) stitch.
The stitches are divided as follows:
6 stitches for the right front border in rib, 29 (32:35) stitches for the right front, 44 (50:56) stitches for the back, 29 (32:35) stitches for the left front, and 6 stitches for the left front border in rib (114 (126:138)) stitches.
Mark the imaginary side seams with stitch markers or safety pins.

LONG HOODED COAT
Sizes S, M, L
Measurements for size S are in front of parentheses: sizes M and L are inside parentheses (M:L). If only one measurement is given, it applies to all sizes.
Style: casual, but not oversized

MATERIALS

- 8 (9:10) balls of Lana Grossa Olympia (109yd/100g; 53% pure new wool, 47% Acrylic) in natural/beige (col. 413)
- US13 (9mm/UK00) circular needles 32in (80cm) long
- Set of US13 (9mm/UK00) double-pointed needles
- Stitch holders or spare needles
- Stitch markers or safety pins

103

Pattern

LONG HOODED COAT

PATTERN DIAGRAM
Measurements in inches (cm)

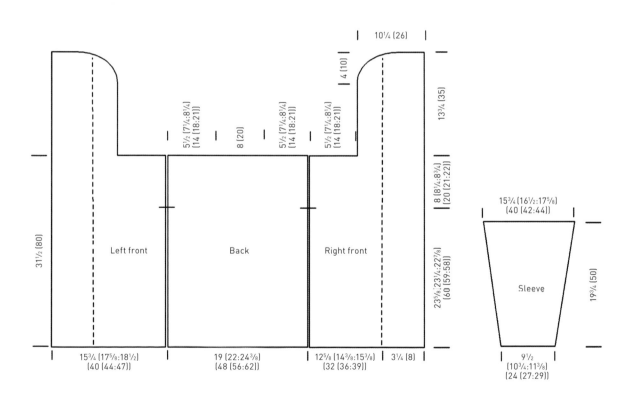

10¼ (26)

4 (10)

13¾ (35)

5½ (7¼:8¼) (14 (18:21))

8 (20)

5½ (7¼:8¼) (14 (18:21))

5½ (7¼:8¼) (14 (18:21))

8 (8¼:8¾) (20 (21:22))

31½ (80)

23⅝ (23¼:22⅞) (60 (59:58))

Left front

Back

Right front

15¾ (17⅝:18½) (40 (44:47))

19 (22:24⅜) (48 (56:62))

12⅝ (14⅜:15⅜) (32 (36:39))

3¼ (8)

15¾ (16½:17⅝) (40 (42:44))

19¾ (50)

Sleeve

9½ (10¾:11⅜) (24 (27:29))

Pockets | On the 2nd right-side row after the border, slip the 12th–24th and 91st–103rd (103rd–115th:115th–127th) stitches onto stitch holders or spare needles. The pockets will be knitted later on these groups of 13 stitches. On the next wrong-side row, cast on 13 stitches above the gaps and continue working in stockinette stitch.

Divide for front and back | When work measures 23⅝ (23¼:22⅞)in (60 (59:58)cm), divide for the armholes and finish the fronts and back separately.

Finish the back | Finish the back first, working in stockinette stitch on the central 44 (50:56) stitches.
When back measures 31½in (80cm), cast off the center 18 stitches and slip the remaining 13 (16:19) stitches at each side onto holders for the shoulders. They will later be knitted together with the shoulder stitches of the fronts.

Finish the fronts | Finish each front separately. Work in stockinette stitch over 29 (32:35) stitches, while continuing in rib on the first or last 6 stitches for the border.
When the work measures 31½in (80cm), slip the 13 (16:19) stitches at the armhole edges onto holders for the shoulders.

Join the shoulder seams | Turn the coat to the wrong side and join one shoulder seam by knitting together 1 stitch of the back and 1 stitch of the front shoulder and cast off. Join the second shoulder seam in the same way.
Alternatively, the shoulder stitches can be grafted together or cast off and sewn up later.

Hood | Pick up the remaining 22 stitches of the right front, 18 stitches from the back neck and 22 stitches of the left front on one needle (62 stitches). Continue working the border in ribbing and work the remaining stitches in stockinette stitch.
Work 10in (25cm), then divide the stitches in two for the back and top of the head. Working outward from the middle on both sides, in every second row cast off 2–3–4–5–6 stitches, so that a total of 20 stitches have been cast off on each half of the hood. Cast off the remaining 11 stitches.
Sew the seam of the hood along the top of the head and down the center back, in one continuous seam.

Pockets | Pick up the 13 stitches from the holders and work 4¾in (12cm) in stockinette stitch and 1¼in (3cm) in rib. Cast off all stitches. Sew the pockets invisibly to the fronts.

Sleeves | The sleeves are knitted in rounds with no seam, on double-pointed needles.
On the set of US13 (9mm) double-pointed needles, cast on 22 (24:26) stitches and distribute evenly. Work 2⅜in (6cm) in rib.
Mark the imaginary seam.
Work the increases by making 1 in the strand between the second and third stitches and between the third-to-last and second-to-last stitches of the round.
Increase at each end of every 7th round a total of 7 times (36 (38:40) stitches on needles).
When sleeve measures 19¾in (50cm), cast off all stitches loosely.

Finishing | Sew in the sleeves. Darn in all the ends.

Snuggle up

TWO-TONE SWEATER WITH BROAD STRIPES

GAUGE
9 stitches and 15 rows in stockinette stitch on US11 (8mm/UK0) needles = 4in (10cm) square.

STITCHES
Stockinette stitch | In rows: right-side rows knit all stitches, wrong-side rows purl all stitches. In rounds: knit all stitches.
Rib border | Knit 2 purl 2 alternately.
Stripes | Sweater: 5 stripes of 6in (15cm): old rose for the ribbed border, then beige, old rose, beige, old rose. Sleeves: old rose for the long cuff, one 6in- (15cm-) stripe in beige and the remainder in old rose.

TO MAKE
Back and front | The sweater is knitted in one piece in rounds up to the armholes. On the US11 (8mm) circular needle, cast on 96 (108:120) stitches in old rose, join into a round and work 6in (15cm) in knit 2 purl 2 rib.
Change to beige and stockinette stitch. Keep an eye on the stripe sequence.

TWO-TONE SWEATER WITH BROAD STRIPES
Sizes S, M, L
Measurements for size S are in front of parentheses: sizes M and L are inside parentheses (M:L). If only one measurement is given, it applies to all sizes.
Style: oversized

MATERIALS
- 4 (5:6) balls of Lana Grossa Bombolo 30 (71yd/50g; 30% mohair, 20% wool, 40% acrylic, 10% nylon) in beige (col. 1) and 6 (7:8) balls in old rose (col. 009)
- US11 (8mm/UK0) circular needle, 32in (80cm) long
- Set of US11 (8mm/UK0) double-pointed needles
- Stitch markers or safety pins
- Spare needles or stitch holders

Divide for front and back | When the work measures 21 (20½:20)in (53 (52:51)cm), divide for the armholes and finish the front and back separately. Divide into 48 (54:60) stitches each for the front and back and change to working in rows. Finish the back first.

Back | Continue in stockinette stitch until back measures 29½in (75cm), then leave the center 20 stitches on a stitch holder or a spare needle. Cast off the 14 (17:20) shoulder stitches on each side loosely.

Front | Now finish the front. When front measures 24¾in (63cm), divide again for the neck and finish each side separately.

Neck opening | Slip the center 12 stitches onto a holder. On every following alternate row, at the neck edge slip off 2 stitches once and 1 stitch twice onto safety pins (14 (17:20) stitches remaining on each side).
When work measures 29½in (75cm), cast off these shoulder stitches on each side.

Shoulder seams | Sew up the shoulder seams.

Roll collar | With a set of US11 (8mm) double-pointed needles and old rose, pick up the stitches from the front and back holders, knitting up 6 stitches from each of the neck edges in between (52 stitches). Work 13¾in (35cm) in knit 2 purl 2 rib, then cast off all stitches loosely.

Sleeves | On the set of double-pointed needles, cast on 24 stitches in old rose and work 9½in (24cm) in knit 2 purl 2 rib in rounds. Change to stockinette stitch and beige. Mark the imaginary sleeve seam.

Sleeve increases | After the long cuff, work increases by making 1 in the strand between the second and third stitches and between the third-to-last and second-to-last stitches of the round.
Increase at each end on every other round 8 (9:10) times in total (40 (42:44) stitches on needles). Remember to change back to old rose after completing a 6in (15cm) stripe in beige. When sleeve measures 21¼in (54cm), cast off all stitches.

Finishing | Sew in the sleeves. Darn in all the ends.

Pattern

PATTERN DIAGRAM
Measurements in inches (cm)

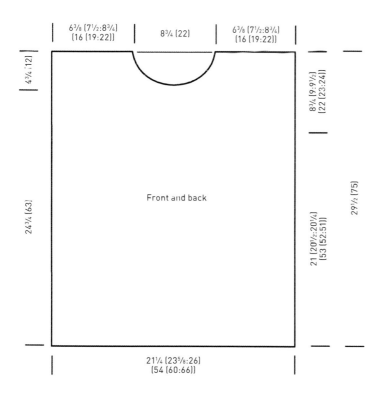

6³⁄₈ (7¹⁄₂:8³⁄₄) (16 (19:22))

8³⁄₄ (22)

6³⁄₈ (7¹⁄₂:8³⁄₄) (16 (19:22))

4³⁄₄ (12)

8³⁄₄ (9:9¹⁄₂) (22 (23:24))

Front and back

24³⁄₄ (63)

21 (20¹⁄₂:20¹⁄₄) (53 (52:51))

29¹⁄₂ (75)

21¹⁄₄ (23⁵⁄₈:26) (54 (60:66))

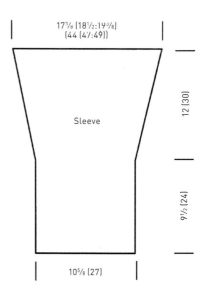

17³⁄₈ (18¹⁄₂:19³⁄₈) (44 (47:49))

Sleeve

12 (30)

9¹⁄₂ (24)

10⁵⁄₈ (27)

Light as air

FLUFFY SWEATER WITH GIANT CABLE

GAUGE

11 stitches and 15 rows in stockinette stitch on US17 (2mm) needles with yarn doubled = 4in (10cm) square.

STITCHES

Stockinette stitch | In rows: right-side rows knit all stitches, wrong-side rows purl all stitches. In rounds: knit all stitches.

Rib border | Knit 2 purl 2 alternately.

Cable pattern | Work from the chart over 30 stitches between the arrows. The figures to the right refer to the right-side pattern rows or rounds. When working in rounds, work all non-cable stitches and rounds in knit: when working in rows, work all wrong-side rows in purl. Starting from the bottom, work rounds 1–54 once, then keep repeating rows or rounds 11–54. Note: only the odd-numbered rounds are shown on the chart; work all the even-numbered rounds or rows as described above, so that a cable is knitted on every 22nd round.

TO MAKE

Work with double yarn (one strand of each).

Back and front | The sweater is knitted in one piece up to the armholes. On the US17 (12mm) circular needle, cast on 120 (132:144) stitches and

FLUFFY SWEATER WITH GIANT CABLE

Sizes S, M, L

Measurements for size S are in front of parentheses: sizes M and L are inside parentheses (M:L). If only one measurement is given, it applies to all sizes.

Style: oversized

MATERIALS

- 11 (12:13) balls of Lana Grossa Alta Moda Super Baby Fine (125yd/25g; 63% pure new wool, 27% alpaca, 10% nylon) in raw white/pale gray mix (col. 07)
- 5 (6:7) balls of Lana Grossa Splendid (182yd/25g; 72% mohair, 21% nylon, 7% metallic) in raw white-silver (col. 12)
- US17 (12mm) circular needle, 32in (80cm) long
- Set of US17 (12mm) double-pointed needles
- Cable needle and stitch holders
- Stitch markers or safety pins

Chart and pattern

FLUFFY SWEATER WITH GIANT CABLE

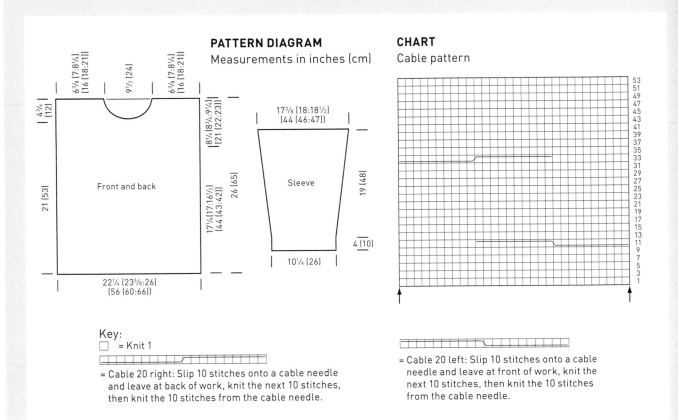

PATTERN DIAGRAM
Measurements in inches (cm)

CHART
Cable pattern

Key:
☐ = Knit 1

= Cable 20 right: Slip 10 stitches onto a cable needle and leave at back of work, knit the next 10 stitches, then knit the 10 stitches from the cable needle.

= Cable 20 left: Slip 10 stitches onto a cable needle and leave at front of work, knit the next 10 stitches, then knit the 10 stitches from the cable needle.

work 4in (10cm) in knit 2 purl 2 rib.
Mark the imaginary side seams between front and back (60 (66:72) stitches for each). Change to stockinette stitch and increase 14 stitches in the front by making 1 in the strand after every 4th stitch.
The front is 14 stitches wider than the back and now consists of 74 (80:86) stitches. The effect of the cable pattern will later make the two parts the same width.
Working the cable pattern over the center

30 stitches, continue in stockinette stitch until work measures 17¼ (17:16⅝)in (44 (43:42)cm).

Divide for front and back | When work measures 17¼ (17:16⅝)in (44 (43:42)cm), divide for the armholes, change to working in rows and finish the back and front separately.

Back | Finish the back first, continuing in stockinette stitch on 60 (66:72) stitches. When work measures 25⅝in (65cm), slip the center

26 stitches onto a holder. Cast off the remaining 17 (20:23) stitches for each shoulder loosely or leave on stitch holders.

Front neck | Now finish the front. When front measures 21¼in (53cm), slip the center 32 stitches onto a holder and finish the right and left neck edges separately.
In every following 2nd row, at the neck edge slip 2 stitches once and 1 stitch twice onto safety pins (17 (20:23) stitches remaining on each side). When work measures 25⅝in (65cm), cast off the shoulder stitches or leave on stitch holders.

Shoulder seams | Sew up the shoulder seams or knit them together.

Roll collar | On a set of double-pointed needles, pick up the stitches from the holders for the front and back neck, picking up 9 stitches in between along each side of the neck (76 stitches).
Work 6in (15cm) stockinette stitch in rounds, continuing the cable pattern from the front. Cut the yarn, turn the sweater to the wrong side, and attach the yarn again. Now on the wrong side, continue in stockinette stitch with the cable pattern. This is so that when the collar is turned down, the knit stitches and cable will appear on the right side.
When the collar measures 13¾in (35cm), cast off all stitches loosely.

Sleeves | The sleeves are long enough to allow the cuffs to be turned up. If you do not want to do this, make the sleeves about 3¼in (8cm) shorter.

Sleeve border | On the set of US17 (12mm) double-pointed needles, cast on 28 stitches and distribute evenly.
Work 4in (10cm) in rounds in knit 2 purl 2 rib.

Change to stockinette stitch and increase 14 stitches evenly in the 1st round (42 stitches on needles). Mark the imaginary sleeve seam. The center 30 stitches will be worked in the cable pattern.

Sleeve increases | Work the increases by making 1 in the strand between the second and third stitches and between the third-to-last and second-to-last stitches of the round, i.e., 2 stitches per round.
Increase at each end of every 6th round a total of 10 (11:12) times (62 (64:66) stitches on needles). When sleeve measures 22in (56cm), in the next round decrease over the 30 stitches of the cable area as follows: knit 1, knit 2 together 14 times, knit 1. Continue in stockinette stitch until sleeve measures 22¾in (58cm), then cast off all stitches.

Finishing | Sew in the sleeves. Darn in all the ends.

To figure out your own sleeve length, measure a suitably sized sweater from your wardrobe from one sleeve-edge up the sleeve, across the back and down to the bottom edge of the other sleeve. Then measure the back width of this sweater, subtract from the total, and divide the remainder by 2.

Easy earth tones

*LONG COAT WITH MULTICOLORED STRIPES
AND CHILD'S SWEATER*

GAUGE

10 stitches and 15 rows in stockinette stitch on
US15 (10mm/UK000) needles with yarn doubled =
4in (10cm) square.

STITCHES

Stockinette stitch | In rows: right-side rows knit
all stitches, wrong-side rows purl all stitches.
In rounds: knit all stitches.

Rib border | Knit 2 purl 2 alternately.

Stripe sequence for back and front of coat |
Work 3¼in (8cm) in rib in red-brown marl,
21 rows light-green marl, 10 rows petrol marl,
14 rows blackberry/gray marl, 4 rows olive marl,
31 rows gray-brown, 4 rows light-green marl,
11 rows petrol/royal marl, 10 rows red-brown
marl, 10 rows blackberry/gray marl, 4 rows
petrol marl, 15 rows light-green marl, 9 rows
gray-brown.

Stripe sequence for coat sleeves | 3¼in (8cm) in
rib in red-brown marl, 4 rows olive marl, 31 rows
gray-brown, 4 rows light-green marl, 11 rows
petrol/royal marl, 10 rows red-brown marl, 10
rows blackberry/gray marl, 4 rows petrol marl,
10 rows light-green marl, 7 rows gray-brown.

LONG KNITTED COAT
Sizes S, M, L

Measurements for size S are in front
of parentheses: sizes M and L are
inside parentheses (M:L). If only one
measurement is given, it applies to
all sizes.

MATERIALS

- Lana Grossa Alta Moda Alpaca: 4
  (5,6) balls in taupe (col. 15), 2 balls
  each in light-green marl (col. 35)
  and gray-brown (col. 10); 2 (3:3)
  balls in red-brown marl (col. 29);
  1 ball each in petrol/royal marl
  (col. 36), blackberry/gray marl (col.
  20), olive marl (col. 43), and petrol
  marl (col. 08)
- US15 (10mm/UK000) circular
  needles, 24 and 32in
  (60 and 80cm) long
- Set of US15 (10mm/UK000)
  double-pointed needles
- Stitch markers or safety pins
- Stitch holders or spare needles
- 5 buttons, ¾in (20mm) diameter

FOR THE COAT

The yarn is worked double, one strand of taupe plus one other color as indicated.

Pockets | Work the pockets first. They will be knitted into the fronts of the coat later. With the shorter US15 (10mm) needles and one strand each of light-green marl and taupe, cast on 18 stitches and work 4¾in (12cm) in stockinette stitch. On the last right-side row, cast off the first two and last two stitches. Slip the remaining 14 stitches onto a stitch holder. Make the second pocket in the same way.

Back and front | The coat is worked in one piece in long rows up to the armholes. With the US15 (10mm) circular needle and one strand of red-brown marl and one of taupe, cast on 88 (100:112) stitches. Begin with a wrong-side row and purl 3, then work in knit 2 purl 2 rib ending with knit 2, then purl the last 3 stitches. Work 2¾in (7cm) in rib as set. Then change to light-green marl and taupe and continue in stockinette stitch. Keep to the stripe sequence. Allocate the stitches as follows: 21 (24:27) stitches for the right front, 46 (52:58) stitches for the back, and 21 (24:27) stitches for the left front. Mark the imaginary side seams with stitch markers or safety pins.

Note: The front border and shawl collar are knitted on later. The border is 1⅝in (4cm) wide. The fronts are ¾in (2cm) narrower than the back, i.e., half the width of the border, so that the buttonholes and buttons will be at the center front. The number of stitches for the fronts is therefore less than half the number for the back.

Attaching pockets | When work measures 15¼in (38cm), on the first olive green row, knit in the

pockets. Knit 5 (6:7) stitches, slip the next 14 stitches onto a stitch holder and knit across the 14 stitches of one pocket, knit the last 2 (4:6) stitches of the right front, the 46 (52:58) stitches of the back and 2 (4:6) stitches of the left front, slip the next 14 stitches onto a stitch holder and knit the 14 stitches of the second pocket, finishing the row with the remaining 5 (6:7) stitches of the left front. The pocket borders will later be knitted on the stitches from the holders. Continue in stockinette stitch, keeping to the stripe sequence.

Decrease for the waist | The coat is slightly shaped. Decreases are worked at both sides. When work measures 22in (56cm), knit together the third-to-last and second-to-last stitches of the right front—i.e., the 19th and 20th stitches for size S, the 22nd and 23rd stitches for size M and the 25th and 26th stitches for size L—the second and third stitches of the back, the third-to-last and second-to-last stitches of the back and the second and third stitches of the left front. (4 stitches decreased per row). Repeat these decreases twice more on every 6th row, (76 (88:100) stitches on the needle). Knit 7 rows, then increase in the next row by knitting into the front and back of the second stitch before and after both side seams. Repeat these increases twice on every 8th row, (88 (100:112) stitches on the needle).

Front neck slope | When work measures 26¾in (68cm), start decreasing for the neck slope on both fronts. On the right front, slip the 3rd stitch, knit 1 and pass slipped stitch over; on the left front knit together the fourth-to-last and third-to-last stitches. Decrease 7 times in all on every 6th row. Remember to divide for the armholes when work measures 31½ (30¾:30)in (80 (78:76)cm).

Divide for fronts and back | When the work measures 31½ (30¾:30)in (80 (78:76)cm), divide for the armholes and finish the fronts and back separately. Continue decreasing at the front neck edge as described above.
The center 46 (52:58) stitches form the back, and the remaining stitches make up the right and left fronts. The number of stitches for the fronts may vary, depending on how many stitches have already been cast off at the neck edge.

Back armhole | Finish the back first. At the beginning of the following rows on each side, cast off 2 stitches twice and 1 stitch once (36 (42:48) stitches.)
Continue in stripe sequence.

Back neck | When work measures 38½in (98cm), cast off the center 12 stitches. On the next row on each side of the neck, cast off 3 stitches at the neck edge. Slip the remaining 9 (12:15) stitches for the shoulders onto holders. They will later be knitted together with the shoulder stitches of the fronts.

Front armholes | Finish the fronts separately. Work the armholes as for the back. Continue decreasing at the neck edge. When work measures 39¼in (100cm), slip the remaining 9 (12:15) stitches onto holders for the shoulders.

Join the shoulder seams | Turn the coat to the wrong side and join one shoulder seam by knitting together 1 stitch of the back and 1 stitch of the front shoulder and casting off one by one. Join the second shoulder seam in the same way. Alternatively, the shoulder stitches can be grafted together or cast off and sewn up later.

Pocket borders | For the pocket borders, work 1⅝in (4cm) in knit 2 purl 2 rib with one strand petrol marl and one strand taupe on the 14 stitches from the holder and cast off all stitches. Sew the side edges of the borders to the fronts. Sew the pockets to the inside of the coat fronts with whipstitch so the stitches cannot be seen on the right side.

Shawl collar | With blackberry/gray marl yarn, pick up 6 stitches up one side of the front neck edge, 4 stitches down from the shoulder seam at the side of the back neck, the 18 cast-off stitches of the back neck, 4 stitches up to the shoulder and another 6 stitches down the other side of the front neck (38 stitches).
Work a wrong-side row in knit 2 purl 2 rib. Turn and work the right-side row in rib. *At the end of the row pick up 2 more stitches on the front edge. Turn and pick up 2 more stitches at the end of the wrong side row *. Repeat from * to * until all the stitches have been picked up as far as the first front decrease (26¾in (68cm) up from the hem). Now pick up stitches along the front edge on each side right down to the hem and work on all the stitches from hem to hem, beginning and ending every right-side row with knit 2 stitches at the hem edge.

Front buttonhole border | When border measures ¾in (2cm), on a right-side row, on the right front 1⅜in (3.5cm) from the hem, cast off 2 stitches for the first buttonhole. Make 4 more buttonholes 6in (15cm) apart, so that there are 5 buttonholes in all. On the following wrong-side row, cast on two stitches above the buttonholes. When the border measures 1⅝in (4cm), cast off all stitches.

Pattern

LONG COAT WITH MULTICOLORED STRIPES

PATTERN DIAGRAM
Measurements in inches (cm)

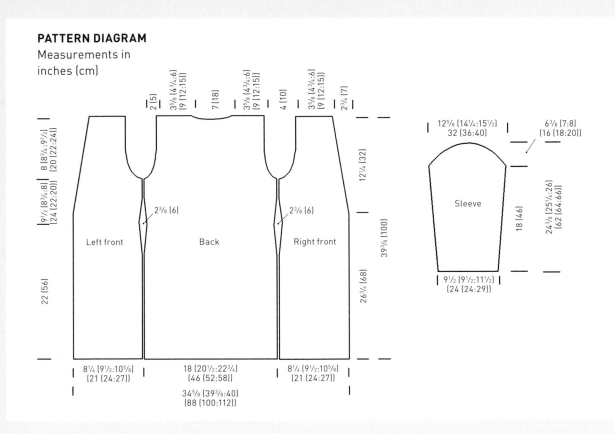

Sleeves | The sleeves are knitted in rounds, with no seam. On the set of US15 (10mm) double-pointed needles, cast on 24 (24:28) stitches in red-brown marl and distribute evenly.
Mark the imaginary seam. Work 2⅜in (6cm) in knit 2 purl 2 rib.
Change to stockinette stitch and olive marl and keep to the stripe sequence.
For size M only: increase 2 stitches, evenly spaced, in the first stockinette stitch round.
Work sleeve increases by making 1 in the strand between the second and third stitches and between the third-to-last and second-to-last stitches of the round, i.e., 2 stitches per round. Increase at each end of the second round of stockinette stitch, then every 7th round, 4 (5:6) times in all, (32 (36:40) stitches on needles).

Shape top | When work measures 18in (46cm), change to working in rows, using two or three needles from the double-pointed needles. When fewer stitches remain, one needle will be enough.

As for the front and back, at the beginning of the following rows on each side, cast off 2 stitches twice and 1 stitch once (22 (26:30) stitches remain).
Then cast off 1–1–0–1 stitches at the beginning of the next 8 rows (2 rows of each), (16 (20:24) stitches remain).
Continue without shaping until work measures 4⅜ (5¼:6)in (11 (13:15)cm) from the start of the armholes. At the beginning of each of the following rows, working 2 rows of each, cast off:
for Size S: 1–2–3 stitches
for Size M: 1–2–4 stitches
for Size L: 1–3–5 stitches.
On the next row, cast off the remaining 4 (6:6) stitches.

Finishing | Sew in the sleeves. Darn in all the ends.

FOR THE CHILD'S SWEATER

The yarn is worked double; one strand of taupe plus one other color as indicated.

Back and front | The sweater is knitted in one piece in rounds up to the armholes.
On US15 (10mm) needles with one strand of petrol/royal marl and one strand of taupe, cast on 80 stitches and work 2⅜in (6cm) in knit 2 purl 2 rib. Then change to stockinette stitch with one strand of light-green marl and one strand of taupe.
Keeping to the stripe sequence of 3⅝in (9cm) in light-green marl with taupe and 3⅝in (9cm) in petrol/royal with taupe, continue in stockinette stitch until work measures 14¼in (36cm).

CHILD'S SWEATER
Size 134–140 (9–10 years)
MATERIALS
- Lana Grossa Alta Moda Alpaca (153yd/50g; 90% alpaca, 5% wool, 5% nylon): 4 balls in taupe (col. 15), 3 balls in light-green marl (col. 35) and 3 balls in petrol/royal marl (col. 36)
- Set of US15 (10mm/UK000) double-pointed needles
- Stitch markers or safety pins
- Stitch holders or spare needles

Pattern

CHILD'S SWEATER

PATTERN DIAGRAM
all measurements in inches (cm)

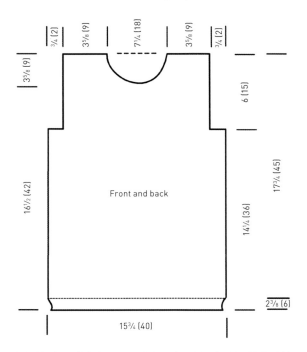

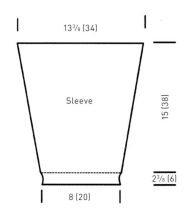

Divide for front and back | When work measures 14¼in (36cm), divide for the armholes and finish the back and front separately. The back and front each consist of 40 stitches. Mark the imaginary side seams. Change to working in rows.

Back armholes | Finish the back first. Cast off 2 stitches at the start of the next 2 rows (36 stitches).
Continue in stripe sequence.

Back neck and shoulders | When work measures 20in (51cm), slip the center 18 stitches onto a holder for the back neck and the outer 9 stitches at each side onto holders or spare needles for the shoulders.
The shoulder stitches will later be knitted together with the shoulder stitches of the fronts. The stitches of the back neck will be continued in the roll collar.

Front armholes | Work the armholes as for the back.
Continue straight until front is 16½in (42cm).

Front neck | When front measures 16½in (42cm), slip the center 12 stitches onto a stitch holder and finish the right and left fronts separately. At the neck edge of every other row, slip 2 stitches once and 1 stitch once onto safety pins for each side of the neck. Continue in stripe sequence on the remaining 9 stitches until front measures 20⅜in (51cm) and slip the stitches onto holders.

Join the shoulder seams | Turn the sweater to the wrong side and join one shoulder seam by knitting together 1 stitch of the back and 1 stitch of the front shoulder and casting off one by one. Join the second shoulder seam in the same way. Alternatively, the shoulder stitches can be grafted together or cast off and sewn up later.

Roll collar | On the set of US15 (10mm) double-pointed needles, with one strand petrol/royal marl and one strand taupe, pick up the 18 stitches of the back neck holder, 6 stitches down the front neck edge, the 18 stitches of the front neck from the holders and 6 stitches up the other side of the neck (48 stitches).
Work 4in (10cm) in knit 2 purl 2 rib on these 48 stitches, then cast off all stitches loosely.

Sleeves | The sleeves are knitted in rounds with no seam. On the set of US15 (10mm) double-pointed needles, with one strand petrol/royal marl and one strand taupe, cast on 20 stitches. Mark the imaginary seam.
Work 2⅜in (6cm) in knit 2 purl 2 rib.
Change to stockinette stitch and one strand light-green marl and one strand taupe and keep to the stripe sequence.

Change color after every 3¾in (9.5cm) as for the front. In order to produce stripes of equal width, the stripes for the sleeve differ from those on the front by 3/16in (0.5cm) per stripe.
Work the sleeve increases by making 1 in the strand between the second and third stitches and between the third-to-last and second-to-last stitches of the round, i.e., 2 stitches per round. Increase at each end of the second round of stockinette stitch, then every 6th round, a further 6 times (34 stitches on needles).
When sleeve measures 17⅜in (44cm), cast off all stitches loosely.

Finishing | Sew in the sleeves. Darn in all the ends.

121

Luxurious lace

PONCHO WITH MATCHING LEG WARMERS

GAUGE

10 stitches and 15 rows in stockinette stitch on US15 (10mm/UK000) needles = 4in (10cm) square.

STITCHES

Stockinette stitch | In rounds: knit all stitches.
Rib border | Knit 2 purl 2 alternately.
Large lace rib | Work from the chart in rounds. Number of stitches divisible by 4. The figures to the right refer to the rounds. The precise allocation of stitches across the width is explained in the instructions. Keep repeating the pattern stitches between the arrows. Starting from the bottom, work rounds 1–24 once, then continue repeating these rounds, working the increased stitches on both sides into the pattern. Slipping the loop of the yarn over means the slipped stitch is extra-long, so it can comfortably stretch over 3 stitches.
Hole pattern for the leg warmers | Work from the chart. The precise allocation of stitches across the width is explained in the instructions. Keep repeating the pattern stitches between the arrows. For clarity, three pattern repeats are shown. Starting from the bottom, keep repeating rounds 1–24.

PONCHO WITH MATCHING LEG WARMERS

One size
Style: generous

MATERIALS

- 12 balls Lion Brand Wool-Ease Thick and Quick (106yd/170g; 80% acrylic, 20% wool) in Blossom for the poncho and 2 balls for the leg warmers
- US15 (10mm/UK000) circular needles, 24, 32, and 40in (60, 80, and 100cm) long
- US15 (10mm/UK000) double-pointed needles for the collar and leg warmers
- Stitch markers or safety pins

FOR THE PONCHO

The poncho is worked in one piece in rounds from the top down, starting with the roll collar in knit 2 purl 2 rib and ending at the bottom hem with a rib border.

The rounds begin between the left arm and the back.

Mark the beginning of the rounds with a stitch marker or safety pin. Change to a longer needle when the number of stitches makes it necessary.

Roll collar | With the set of US15 (10mm) double-pointed needles, cast on 60 stitches and work 9½in (24cm) in knit 2 purl 2 rib.

Stitch division for fast increases | Divide the stitches into four areas of 15 stitches. Mark the four areas so you can see them more easily. Work 2 rounds of stockinette stitch, then begin increasing. As shown in the chart, on every 4th round increase 2 stitches per "quarter," i.e., 8 stitches per round. The chart shows a quarter of a poncho. When 8 stitches have been increased in a quarter, a new pattern repeat will have been produced at each side.

Increase 8 times in every 4th round, so that after working 8 vertical pattern repeats, two new pattern repeats will have been produced at each side of each quarter (31 stitches per quarter, 124 stitches per round).

Change to slower increases | After working 8 vertical repeats, increase as shown in the chart 4 more times on every 8th round, by working yarn over needle after the first stitch and before the last stitch of each quarter.

This will produce 39 stitches per quarter (156 stitches per round).

Each quarter will now divide into knit 2, 9 repeats of 4 stitches, knit 1.

Continue without shaping | Continue on these 156 stitches as described above until the poncho measures 32in (81cm), 9½in (24cm) collar and 22½in (57cm) in pattern).

Bottom border | When poncho measures 32in (81cm), work 2in (5cm) in knit 2 purl 2 rib, then cast off all stitches loosely.

Finishing | Darn in all the ends.

FOR THE LEG WARMERS

The leg warmers are knitted in one piece in rounds from the bottom up, starting with a rib border at the ankle and ending with a rib border at the knee.

Mark the start of the rounds with a stitch marker or safety pin.

On a set of US15 (10mm) double-pointed needles, cast on 20 stitches and work 4in (10cm) in knit 2 purl 2 rib.

Next round: change to stockinette stitch and increase 8 stitches evenly over the round (28 stitches). Work 1 round stockinette stitch.

Next and following rounds, work from the chart, repeating rounds 1–4 until the work measures 10in (25cm). The stitches between the arrows will be repeated 7 times per round. On the next 4 rounds, knit into the front and back of the last stitch (32 stitches).

There will now be 8 repeats per round instead of 7.

When work measures 15¾in (40cm), after a 4th round of the chart, work 1 more round in stockinette stitch.

Finish the leg warmer with 3¼in (8cm) in knit 2 purl 2 rib and cast off all stitches loosely.

Finishing | Darn in all the ends.

Make a second leg warmer in the same way.

Charts and pattern

PONCHO WITH MATCHING LEG WARMERS

CHART
Large lace pattern for poncho

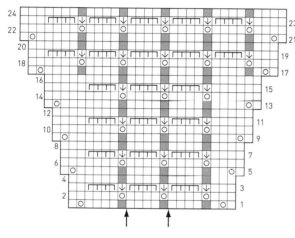

CHART
Hole-pattern leg warmers

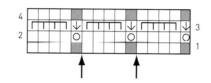

Key:

☐ = Knit 1 stitch

Ⓞ = 1 yarn over

↓ = 1 new yarn over and drop the yarn over from the previous row.

▨ = No stitch. Ignore when knitting.

⌐⊓⊓⊓⊓ = Work over 4 stitches: slip 1 knitwise, knit the next 3 stitches and pass the slipped stitch over the 3 knit stitches (= 3 stitches).

PATTERN DIAGRAM FOR PONCHO
Measurements in inches (cm)

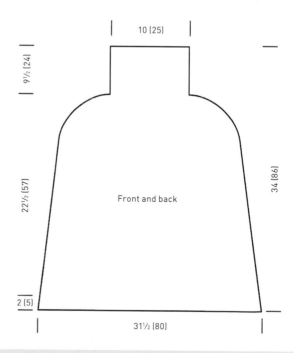

Basic techniques

WHETHER YOU'RE NEW TO KNITTING OR BRUSHING UP YOUR
SKILLS, THIS EASY-TO-FOLLOW GUIDE TO BASIC TECHNIQUES WILL
HELP YOU ACHIEVE GREAT RESULTS EVERY TIME.

Casting on

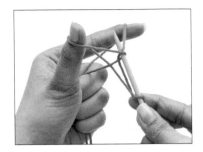

1 Make a slipknot around the needle, leaving a very long yarn tail. Hold the needle in your right hand, then loop the yarn tail over your left thumb and the ball yarn end around your left index finger. Hold both strands in place in the palm of your left hand.

2 Insert the tip of the needle from under and up through the loop on your thumb.

3 Wrap the tip of the needle around the loop on your forefinger from right to left, then use it to pull the yarn through the loop on your thumb.

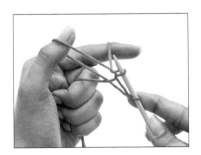

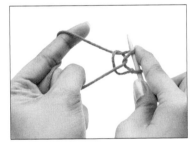

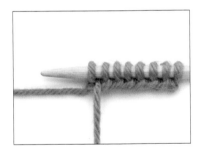

4 Slip your thumb out of the loop.

5 Pull both yarn ends gently, to tighten the cast-on loop on the needle. Slide the new stitch up closer to the first slipknot stitch.

6 Loop the yarn around your thumb again and cast on another stitch by repeating Steps 2 to 6. Continue casting on until you have as many stitches as you need.

Casting off knitwise

1 Knit the first two stitches. Then insert the left needle into the first stitch and pull it up and over the second stitch, until it is off the right needle.

2 Knit one more stitch, then repeat Step 1 to remove the stitch before it. Continue in the same way until only one stitch remains on the needle.

3 Cut the yarn, leaving either a tail of 8 in (20 cm) to be darned in later, or a much longer tail to use for a future seam. Pass the yarn end through the remaining loop and pull it tight.

Slipping stitches off the needle

Using a stitch holder: If you are setting stitches aside to work on later, slip them carefully onto a suitable-sized stitch holder. Your instructions should tell you whether to cut the yarn or keep it attached to the ball.

Using a length of yarn: If you don't have a stitch holder, you can use cotton yarn. Using a large tapestry needle, pull the yarn through the stitches as you slip them off the knitting needle. Knot the ends of the cotton yarn together.

Slipping stitches

Slipping stitches purlwise

1 Always slip stitches purlwise unless you are instructed otherwise. Insert the right needle into the front of the loop on the left needle, as if to work a purl stitch.

2 Slide the stitch onto the right needle without working it. The slipped stitch now sits on the right needle, with the right side of the loop at the front and the yarn at the back of the work.

Slipping stitches knitwise

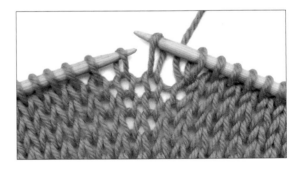

1 Only slip stitches knitwise if you are working decreases or if instructed to do so. Insert the right needle from right to left through the front of the loop on the left needle.

2 Slide the stitch off the left needle and onto the right needle without working it. The slipped stitch now sits on the right needle, with the left side of the loop at the front, unlike the worked stitches next to it.

Reading charts

Some knitters prefer charts to written patterns because they are easy to read, and because the visual patterns of the stitch repeats can be easier to memorize. The number of stitches to cast on is usually indicated on the chart. If not, you can calculate the cast-on. Count the number of stitches in the repeat and cast on a multiple of that number, plus any end stitches outside the repeat.

Each square represents one stitch and each horizontal line represents a row. After casting on, work from the bottom of the chart up. Read odd-numbered rows (usually right-side rows) from right to left, and even numbered rows (usually wrong-side rows) from left to right. Work the edge stitches, then work the stitches inside the repeat as many times as instructed. Some symbols mean one thing in the right-side (RS) row and another in the wrong-side (WS) row. When you have worked all the rows, start again at the bottom to begin the "row repeat" once more.

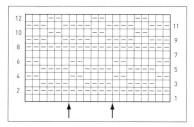

Measuring gauge

Before you start a project, knit a swatch so you can make sure you are knitting the correct stitch size (gauge) for your pattern. If your finished work doesn't have the correct gauge, the finished item may not fit.

1 Using the recommended needle size, knit a swatch about 5 in (13 cm) square. Lay it flat and insert two pins 4 in (10 cm) apart. Count the number of stitches between the pins.

2 Now count the number of rows to 4 in (10 cm) in the same way. If there are fewer rows and stitches than in the instructions, use smaller needles. If there are more, try larger needles. For your project, use the needle size that best matches the correct gauge.

Altering patterns

You can alter the length of garment patterns worked in plain garter or stockinette stitch, but avoid altering armholes, necklines, and the tops of sleeve heads. Since sleeves and some bodies have shaping, these must be adjusted, too. Here's how to lengthen a sleeve.

1 Photocopy, draw, or trace the original pattern diagram. Write the new required length on your copy, for example, 19 in (48 cm).
2 Find the number of rows to 4 in (10 cm) in the gauge note. Divide that number by 4 (10) to calculate the number of rows there are in 1 in (cm). For example, if there were 30 rows per 4 in (10 cm), there would be 4.5 rows per 1 in (3 rows per 1 cm).
3 Multiply the required new length by the number of rows in 1 in (cm). The answer is the total number of rows in the new length—for example, 19 (in) x 4.5 (sts per in) = 85.5 rows (48 (cm) × 3 (rows per cm) = 144 rows).
4 Any increasing will also have to be recalculated. From the pattern, note the number of stitches to cast on at the cuff and how many there will be on the needle just before starting the underarm shaping. (This figure is often shown at the end of the instructions for the increases.)
5 Subtract the smallest number from the largest number of stitches to be increased. Divide the answer by two (because a sleeve has two sides) to give the number of stitches to increase on each side. For example: 114 - 60 = 54 stitches. 54 ÷ 2 = 27. So 27 stitches would be increased at each side.
6 To calculate the number of rows between each increase, divide the new number of rows found in Step 3 by the number of increases worked out in Step 5. If the answer is a fraction, round it down to a whole number. For example: 85.5 ÷ 27 = 3.1 (144 ÷ 27 = 4.22). So, you would increase one stitch each side every 3 (4) rows. Knit the remaining rows straight before doing the underarm cast-offs.

Increasing

Knit into front and back of stitch

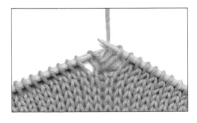 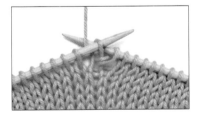 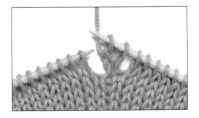

1 Knit the stitch, but do not slip it off the left needle. Insert the right needle through the back of the loop from right to left.

2 Wrap the yarn around the right needle, draw the yarn through to make a second stitch, then drop the old stitch off the left needle.

3 In this way, two knit stitches are created from one and the row is increased by one stitch.

"Make-one" left cross increase on a knit row

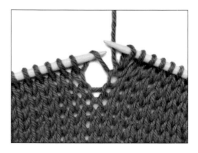

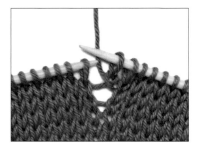

1 With the left needle, pick up the horizontal strand between the stitch just knitted and the next stitch, as shown.

2 Wrap the yarn around the tip of the right needle and draw the yarn through the lifted loop. This is called knitting through the back of the loop.

3 There is now an extra stitch in the row. Knitting through the back of the loop creates a twist that closes up the hole that a new stitch would otherwise have created.

Yarn over between knit stitches

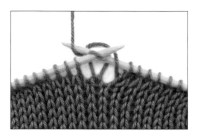

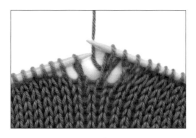

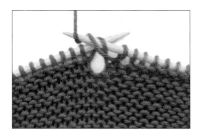

1 Bring the yarn to the front between the needles. Take the yarn over (yo) the top of the right needle to the back, then knit the next stitch.

2 When the knit stitch is complete, the yarn over is correctly formed on the right needle with the right leg of the loop at the front.

3 In the next row, when you reach the yarn over, purl it through the front of the loop in the usual way. This creates a hole under the purl stitch.

Decreasing

Knit two together

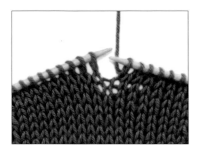 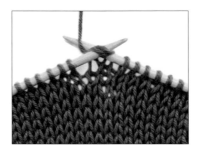 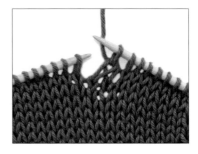

1 Insert the right needle knitwise from left to right through the second, and then the first stitch on the left needle.

2 Wrap the yarn around the right needle, draw the yarn through both loops at the same time and slide both loops onto the right needle.

3 This makes two stitches into one. The completed stitch slants to the right.

Slip one, knit one, pass slipped stitch over

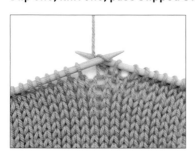 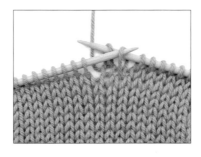 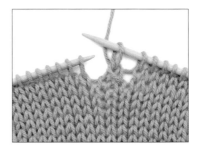

1 Slip the first stitch from the left needle knitwise (see page 130). Knit the next stitch.

2 Pick up the slipped stitch with the tip of the left needle. Pass it over the new knit stitch and off the right needle.

3 The two stitches have become one stitch. The completed decrease slants to the left.

Cables

Cables are usually knitted in stockinette stitch on a reverse stockinette stitch (or garter stitch) background. They are made by crossing two, three or more stitches over other stitches in the row. Here the technique is illustrated with the cable 4 front and cable 4 back cables, which are crossed on every sixth row.

Cable 4 front

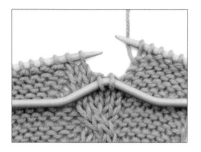 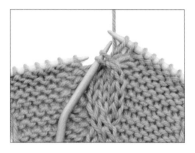 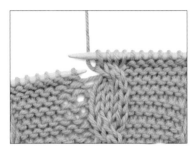

1 Work to the position of the four stockinette stitches that form the cable. Slip the first two knit stitches that form the cable onto a cable needle. With the cable needle at the front, knit the next two stitches on the left needle.

2 Next, knit the two stitches from the cable needle.

3 This creates a cable crossing that slants to the left, which is why a front cable is sometimes called a left cable.

Cable 4 back

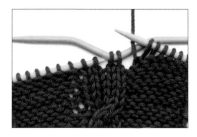 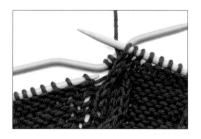 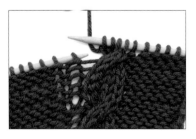

1 Work as for Step 1 of Cable 4 front, but hold the cable needle with the slipped stitches at the back of the work. Knit the next two stitches as normal.

2 Then knit the two stitches from the cable needle.

3 This creates a cable crossing that slants to the right. For this reason, a back cable is also known as a right cable.

Horizontal inset pocket

1 Make the pocket lining before you knit the garment piece. It must be two stitches wider than the cast-off for the pocket. After working the last row, leave on the needle or slip onto a stitch holder.

2 With the right side facing, work the main piece to the position of the pocket opening. Cast off knitwise the stitches for the pocket opening (see page 129), then knit to the end of the row.

3 Turn and purl back to one stitch from the pocket position. Take the needle with the lining stitches in your left hand and purl the last main stitch and the first lining stitch together.

4 Purl across the lining stitches. Purl the last stitch of the pocket together with the first one on the left needle. Finish working the main piece.

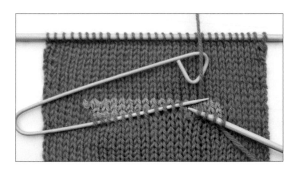

5 As an alternative to Step 2, you could slip the opening stitches, without casting off, onto a stitch holder. Then you can knit an edging to the pocket later on.

6 To make up the piece, sew the lining to the main piece with whipstitch, taking care not to pull the stitches too tight. This example has a contrasting colorway, but the lining would usually be made in the main yarn.

Pom-poms

1 On a piece of cardboard, draw two circles 3in (8cm) in diameter, then two circles of 1in (2.5cm) diameter in the center of each. Cut out the circles so that you have two ring shapes. Now cut a few 1yd (1m) lengths of yarn and wind them together. Put the rings exactly on top of one another and start winding the yarn through the rings as shown.

2 When the first ball of yarn runs out, make another and continue winding. When the hole is filled, insert the tip of a pair of scissors between the pieces of cardboard and start to cut the yarn around the outside of the ring.

3 Continue cutting until all the wound strands of yarn have been cut along the outer rim of the ring. Now slide a long, doubled strand of yarn between the two pieces of cardboard, then wrap and knot it tightly around the center of the pom-pom.

4 Carefully remove the pieces of cardboard. Shake the pom-pom to fluff it up and trim into shape if necessary. Don't cut off the tie strands, as they can be used to sew on the pom-pom or hang it up. You can plump up your pom-pom even more by suspending it in steam for a few minutes (hang it off a knitting needle for safety).

Working on a set of five double-pointed needles

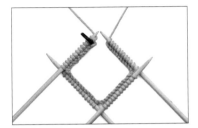

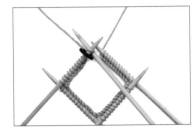

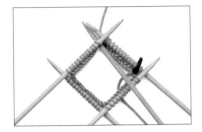

1 Cast on the stitches on one needle, then distribute them evenly over four needles. Insert a marker between the first two stitches of the first round. Form the four needles into a square, taking care not to twist the cast-on row.

2 Use the fifth needle to knit with. Work the first stitch of each needle tightly so that there are no gaps where you change from one needle to the next.

3 When you have knitted all the stitches off the first needle, use the empty needle to work the stitches on the second needle. Continue working in this way, slipping the stitch marker from the left needle to the right when it is reached.

Finishing

Picking up stitches along a side edge

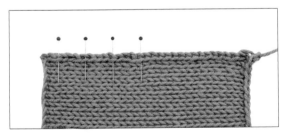

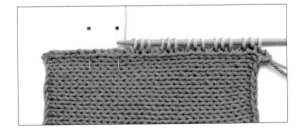

1 For lightweight or medium-weight yarn, pick up about three stitches for every four row-ends. On the right side of the knitting, place a pin on the first of every four row-ends, as shown here.

2 Insert the needle in the center of the edge stitch and knit the stitches as you would when picking up along a cast-on edge. Skip every fourth row-end and remove pins before picking up stitches.

Cast-off horizontal buttonhole

1 On a knit row, work as far as the position of the buttonhole. Work two more stitches, then cast off knitwise however many stitches you need for the buttonhole (see page 129). When the last cast-off loop is on the right needle, slip the first stitch on the left needle onto the right needle and pass the cast-off loop over it. Knit to the end of the row. Turn, and work as far as the buttonhole.

2 Drop the left needle (use a point protector to retain stitches if necessary). Hold the yarn and the right needle in your right hand. With your left thumb pointing down, pick up the yarn from behind, then wind your thumb to the right in a counterclockwise circle so the yarn crosses near the needle. Insert the right needle into the front thumb loop.

3 Bring your left index finger from beneath, catching the yarn. Take the yarn left behind the needle, then wind it to the right, over the needle.

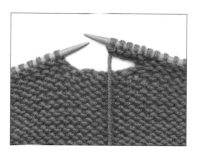

4 Slip the thumb loop onto the right needle. Hold the loop with your right index finger and tighten the yarn with your left hand, making sure the loop goes all around the needle. Repeat for each cast-on stitch and knit to the end of the row.

5 The horizontal buttonhole is finished.

Joining seams

Mattress stitch

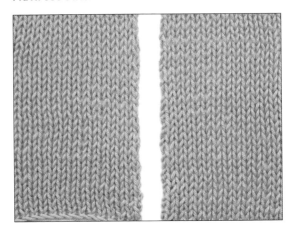

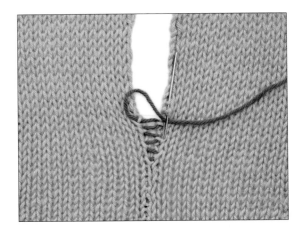

1 Ribbing and stockinette stitch pieces can be sewn together almost invisibly with mattress stitch. Place the two pieces next to each other with the right sides facing up.

2 Insert the needle from the front through the center of the first knit stitch on one piece of work, then up through the center of the stitch two rows above. Repeat on the other piece. Work from the bottom up, pulling the edges together.

Grafting

Grafting can be used to join both cast-off edges and rows of stitches that have not been cast off.

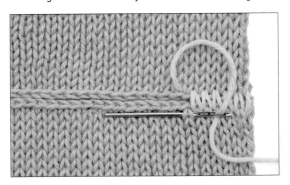

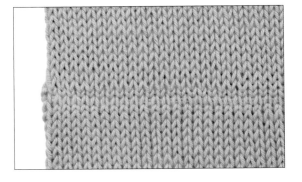

1 Place the pieces edge to edge with the right sides up. Work from right to left, inserting the needle through the stitches as shown.

2 If you work in a matching yarn as shown here, the seam blends in completely. The result will look like a continuous piece of knitting.

Blocking

When blocking (finishing a piece by steaming or pressing), always refer to your yarn label before you start. Textured patterns such as garter stitch, ribbing, and cables should be wet blocked or steamed very gently, so that you don't stretch or squash the pattern.

Wet blocking

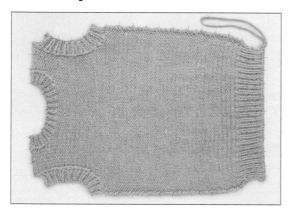

If the yarn allows it, wet blocking is the best way to even out your knitting. Wet or wash the piece in lukewarm water. Squeeze out gently, then roll up in a dry towel to squeeze out more moisture. Pin the piece into shape on a layer of dry towels covered with a sheet and leave to dry.

Steam blocking

Only steam block if your yarn allows. Pin the piece into shape, then place a damp cloth on top. Use a warm iron to create steam, barely touching the damp cloth. Do not press the iron down on the knitting, and avoid any textured areas such as cables and ribbing. Leave the pins in place until the piece has dried completely.

About the author

Helgrid van Impelen has a degree in clothing technology; she is a fashion designer and a knitting and crochet junkie. Some years ago, after having abandoned craft activities for a long period during a busy phase in her career, she rediscovered knitting and crochet as the perfect way to relieve stress. Gradually, one book led to another, and writing craft books now takes up the major part of her professional activities.

Thanks

Thanks from the author | Grateful thanks to all the lovely busy knitters around me, especially to my mother, my aunt, and my friend Anja. In addition, my thanks go to the firm of Lana Grossa and especially to Christine Lenz, who is always calm, often inspires me, and without whose unstinting help, many things would not be possible.

Thanks from the publisher | DK Verlag wishes to thank Lana Grossa (www.lanagrossa.de) for their support with the materials, Katja, Gina and Cora for their hard work during the photo shoots, Eva and Marcus for their photogenic flat and Irmi Eisenbarth of the Café "Das GaumenSpiel" (Franz-Joseph-Str. 30, 80801 Munich), where we were given permission to shoot some of the photos.

Photography and styling Katja Schubert, except for:
Photos p. 8–9 and 128–141 DK Verlag
Styling of models Gina Pieper
Hair and makeup Corina Friedrich
Models Anne Wunderlich, Ana Saraiva Ludwig, Viktoria Fischer
Charts Edeltraut Söll
Pattern diagrams Helgrid van Impelen
Illustrations Derhajoe/Dreamstime (Schaf),
Dmstudio/Dreamstime (Wollknäuel), DeCe/Shutterstock (Schere)
Editing Anna Gülicher-Loll
Layout, typography, realisation Bettina Hoche

For DK Verlag
Publisher Monika Schlitzer
Editorial management Caren Hummel
Project monitoring Katharina May
Production management Dorothee Whittaker
Production coordination Arnika Marx
Production Inga Reinke

For DK UK
Translation from German Rae Walter in association with
First Edition Translations Ltd., Cambridge, UK
Editor Rona Skene
Project Editor Kathryn Meeker
Senior Art Editor Glenda Fisher
Design Assistant Philippa Nash
Jacket Designer Harriet Yeomans
Senior Producer, Pre-Production Tony Phipps
Producer Che Creasy
Creative Technical Support Sonia Charbonnier
Managing Editor Stephanie Farrow
Managing Art Editor Christine Keilty

For DK US
Consultant: Jennifer Wendell Kosek
Senior Editor: Margaret Parrish
Managing Editor: Lori Hand
US Publisher: Mike Sanders

First American Edition, 2015
Published in the United States by DK Publishing
345 Hudson Street, New York, New York 10014

Copyright © 2016 Dorling Kindersley Limited
Translation copyright © Dorling Kindersley Limited, 2016
DK, a Division of Penguin Random House LLC
16 17 18 19 20 10 9 8 7 6 5 4 3 2 1
001–294125–Sept/2016

A catalog record for this book is available from the Library of Congress.
ISBN: 978-1-4654-5398-3

Printed and bound in China

All images © Dorling Kindersley Limited
For further information see: www.dkimages.com

A WORLD OF IDEAS:
SEE ALL THERE IS TO KNOW

www.dk.com